Real Classroom Makeovers

Practical Ideas for Early Childhood Classrooms

by Rebecca Isbell and Pamela Evanshen

Special Thanks

During the development of this book, many early childhood teachers have invited us into their classrooms. They have met with us, collaborated on plans, and assisted in renovating their spaces. This process was lengthy and often necessitated meeting in the later afternoon, and on evenings and weekends. It is with their help and support that this project was possible and the creation of these amazing classrooms evolved.

The following early childhood educators were instrumental in these makeovers:

Kathy Arney – Kindergarten Teacher

Angie Baker – Assistant Principal

Lisa Baxter – PreK Teacher

Kathy Carter – Preschool Teacher

Aaron Clark – Preschool Teacher

Lauren Click –Kindergarten Teacher

Elesha Cornett – Kindergarten Teacher

Sherry Egan – PreK Teacher

Daniela Floresguerra – Kindergarten Teacher

Laura Guthrie – Kindergarten Teacher

Ashley Hobbs –Kindergarten Teacher

Janice Irvin – Kindergarten Teacher

Sara Lewis – PreK Teacher

Jennifer Lingerfelt – PreK Coordinator

Darrellen Lodien – Lead Preschool Teacher

Joy Matson – Preschool Teacher

Yvelle Mull – Kindergarten Teacher

Mary Myron – Kindergarten Teacher

Debra Oglesby – Preschool Teacher

Kathy Osborn – Even Start Family Literacy Program Director

Gloria Reilly – Preschool Teacher

Jenny Seeley – PreK Teacher

Sharon Slagle – PreK Teacher

Yolanda Steadman – Kindergarten Teacher

Becky Taylor – Child Care Director

Krista Turner – Director, Little Bucs

Jackie Vaughn – Preschool Teacher

Beverly Wiginton – Child Study Center Director

Dedication

We would like to dedicate this book to all the creative, and hardworking early childhood teachers who work with young children each day.

Rebecca Isbell

Pamela Evanshen

Also by Rebecca Isbell

The Complete Learning Center Book, Revised

The Complete Learning Spaces Book for Infants and Toddlers, with Christy Isbell

Early Learning Environments That Work, with Betty Exelby

The Inclusive Learning Center Book, with Christy Isbell

Sensory Integration, with Christy Isbell

Tell It Again!, with Shirley Raines

Tell It Again! 2, with Shirley Raines

Also by Pamela Evanshen

A Room to Learn: Rethinking Classroom Environments, with Janet Faulk

Acknowledgments

Many special people have contributed to the development of this book. First, Julia Herwig has been a wonderful editor and organizer of materials. We greatly appreciate her making the content flow smoothly so it communicates the ideas as clearly as we intended. Helen Lane and Charity Hensley, doctoral fellows in our Early Childhood Education PhD Program, were always available to work in many different ways, from setting up areas to filling in missing references. They are wonderful people to work with and always complete tasks with enthusiasm. Andrea Valentine, graduate assistant, has been involved from the beginning of the project. Her knowledge and well-organized thinking have enabled her to make significant contributions to many different aspects of our book.

We were blessed to work with a talented photographer, Michael Talley, who has traveled throughout our region taking before, after, and sometimes many additional pictures. His visuals help you see what occurred in the makeovers and help you understand the elements that were added.

Matthew Allen has drawn the layouts of the spaces, which include the features of the environment and the materials that were planned. These visuals provide another way of looking at the space and of understanding the steps in the planning process.

An additional thanks to Clarissa Willis and Robyn Clark who helped us secure some of the materials from Kaplan Early Learning Company that were used to enrich several of the amazing classroom environments.

Our deep appreciation goes to these talented and cooperative people who helped make this book possible.

Real Classroom Makeovers

Practical Ideas for Early Childhood Classrooms

Rebecca Isbell and Pamela Evanshen

Gryphon House, Inc.
Lewisville, NC

Published by Gryphon House, Inc.
PO Box 10, Lewisville, NC 27023
800.638.0928; 877.638.7576 (fax)

Visit us on the web at www.gryphonhouse.com.

Cover photograph courtesy of Michael Talley.

Library of Congress Cataloging-in-Publication Data

Isbell, Rebecca T.
 Real classroom makeovers : practical ideas for early childhood classrooms
/ Rebecca Isbell, Pam Evanshen.
   p. cm.
 ISBN 978-0-87659-378-3 (pbk.)
1. Early childhood education. 2. Classroom environment. 3. Creative
teaching. I. Evanshen, Pamela. II. Title.
LB1139.23.I73 2012
372.21--dc23
                    2011049983

Bulk Purchase

Gryphon House books are available for special premiums and sales promotions as well as for fund-raising use. Special editions or book excerpts also can be created to specifications. For details, contact the Director of Marketing at Gryphon House.

Disclaimer

TABLE OF CONTENTS

Introduction 7

Chapter 1
The Environment Matters: Design Elements to Consider 9
Beauty in Everyday Environments 9
The Impact of Light 13
Sounds Make a Difference 13
A Place for Everything, Everything in Its Place 15
A Secure and Supportive Environment.........................16
Valuing Diversity in the Classroom 18
Setting Up Appropriate Learning Environments.............19

Chapter 2
The Process of Planning for Successful Change 23
Creating the Vision...23
Developing a Plan...25
Introducing a New Feature 27

Chapter 3
Low-Cost, Big-Impact Changes......29
Decluttering...29
Small Changes 30
Teacher's Space 32

Chapter 4
Building a Sense of Community in the Classroom....................................35
Creating a Welcoming and Inviting Entrance 36
Developing a Sense of Place...37
Valuing Each Member of the Community 38
Having Effective Group Time 39
Learning About and Practicing Responsibility...............40
Identifying Personal Spaces for Children 41
Providing Choices for Individual Work...........................42
Working in Small Groups 42

Chapter 5
Real Classroom Makeovers 43
The Importance of Play...43
Real Classroom Makeovers Support
    Children's Play 45
Literacy Centers/Areas 45
    Library Canopy...46
    Library Tent 49
    Literacy Area 53
Manipulatives/Building...57
    Construction...57
    Blocks 61
    Manipulatives 65
Math and Science..69
    Water 69
    Math 74
    Science 78
Art and Music..82
    Music and Performance...................................82
    Art Studio 87
Dramatic Play..92
    Home Living 92
    Fire Station 97
    Restaurant 101
Community Meeting...106
    Gathering Place 106
Nurturing Environment..111
    Welcome Area 111
    Calming Place..117

Chapter 6
Early Learning Standards and the Classroom Environment................123
Early Learning Standards 123
The Unique Needs of Children 124
Adapting the Environment for All Learners 126

Chapter 7
The Amazing (and Real) Classroom
Makeover Adventure 127

The Adventure...127
Description of the Classroom 127
Developing a Vision with an Initial Teacher Interview....128
The Change Process 129
The First Element of Design Considered:
  Beauty in Everyday Environments 129
  Plan of Action 129
The Next Element of Design Considered:
  A Place for Everything, Everything in Its Place 130
  Setting up Appropriate Learning Environments......130
  Plan of Action 130
Teacher Interview and Reflection on the
  Learning Environment 130
Art 131
  Plan of Action 131
  Standards Addressed During Play in the
    Art Center 132
Books 133
  Plan of Action 133
  Standards Addressed During Play in the
    Book Center.....................................134
Blocks 135
  Plan of Action 135
  Standards Addressed During Play in the
    Block Center....................................136
Gathering Place 137
  Plan of Action....................................137

  Standards Addressed During Play in the
    Gathering Area 138
Home Living...139
  Plan of Action....................................139
  Standards Addressed During Play in the
    Home Living Center..............................139
Science 140
  Plan of Action....................................140
  Standards Addressed During Play in the
    Science Center 141
Writing 142
  Plan of Action....................................142
  Standards Addressed During Play in the
    Writing Center..................................143
Summary...144
Teacher Comments After the Makeover 145
  Before the Beginning of School............................145
  Midyear 145
  Final Reflection 147

References..................................149

Classroom Evaluation Checklist 151

Index 153

The environment influences how young children learn, behave, interact, and participate in an early childhood classroom. An effective environment for young children is inviting, interesting, challenging, and nurturing. It engages children in real-life experiences and meaningful activities. The environment also influences how teachers feel about the classroom and how they view their involvement with children. An organized environment that is beautiful and clearly communicates the wonderful learning opportunities available to children makes it easier for teachers to conduct authentic observations of young children's participation, collaboration, language interactions, and developing skills. In this environment, it is clearly visible that young children live in a well-designed classroom and actively participate in appropriate activities and meaningful interactions with adults and other children.

An organized environment that is beautiful and clearly communicates the wonderful learning opportunities available to children makes it easier for teachers to conduct authentic observations of young children's participation, collaboration, language interactions, and developing skills.

Real early childhood environments can range from dark basements to new buildings designed specifically for young children. Each classroom has features that cannot be changed, such as windows and electrical outlets. At the same time, each classroom offers unique challenges and opportunities. With a clear vision of how these places can function, it is possible to transform any environment into a wonderful place for young children and their teachers to grow and learn together.

This book provides visual examples of changes that are possible in real preschool, PreK, and kindergarten classrooms. Most of the makeovers in Chapter 5 focus on a specific classroom area or learning center. The final chapter reflects the process of a complete classroom makeover. Each makeover project begins in collaboration with the classroom teachers, who share needs and expectations for their classrooms based upon their knowledge of the young children with whom they work. Photographs visually demonstrate the space at the beginning of the makeover process and follow the implementation of the plan for change. Additional pictures and explanations further support the rationale for the changes and help the reader understand how these changes impact the environment and, ultimately, how the changes help children focus on the learning that takes place in this area. The classroom transformations are amazing and demonstrate the capabilities of many very creative and hardworking early childhood teachers. The comments from children working and playing in the new spaces clearly communicate their interest and excitement about the new possibilities.

Chapter 1

The Environment Matters

DESIGN ELEMENTS TO CONSIDER

Beauty in Everyday Environments

Discovering the shadows of the trees on the playground, noticing a smooth blue pebble, or observing a woven wall hanging are all ways to help children see and appreciate the everyday beauty that surrounds them. You also can arrange your classroom environment so it provides many ways for children to enjoy beautiful materials and treasures in their space. Simple displays of natural materials in the classroom provide a place to see, touch, and enjoy items such as an empty hornets' nest, a clear container of pebbles, pinecones, a mossy plant, or bark from a tree. Talking with the children about the unique features of these collections extends their ideas and expands their vocabulary, empowering them to communicate their thoughts.

Building Materials

1. A basket to display building materials

Natural Materials

2. A novel mobile made with natural and craft materials

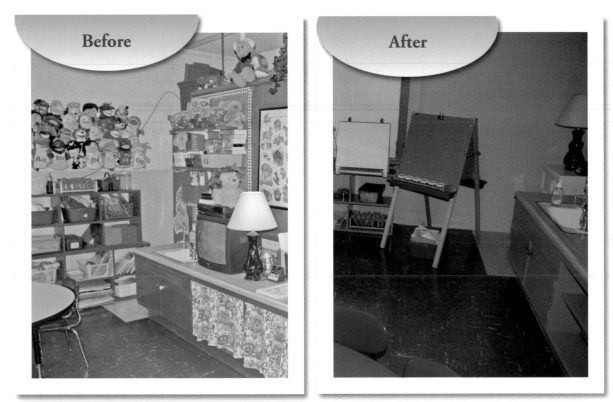

Before

After

Color has a tremendous effect on the atmosphere of an early childhood classroom. For many years, primary colors on the wall, brightly colored toys, and bold, colorful displays filled classrooms for young children. Since that time, we have learned a lot about the impact of color in a classroom. The educators in the Reggio Emilia programs in Italy use color in a very different way: Light-colored walls provide a background for the children's work. In their schools, the color comes from the artwork, materials, and panels that reflect the children's learning and activities. This way of using color has had a tremendous impact on many early childhood programs.

Painting is one of the quickest and least expensive ways to change your classroom environment. By painting the walls a neutral color, the focus of the space is on the children's work rather than on the color of the walls. Add color to the space with displays and selected materials in such a way that the additions enhance the organization of the classroom. For example, add a colorful arrangement of art materials and displays of the children's artwork in the Art Studio area. Other possible additions of color are natural materials, fabric, murals, wall hangings, pillows, labels, and aesthetically pleasing decorations. These items also add textural interest to the classroom and invite children to use their sense of touch to explore the classroom environment.

Displays of artwork inspire children to try new art techniques or simply expose them to art created in different ways.

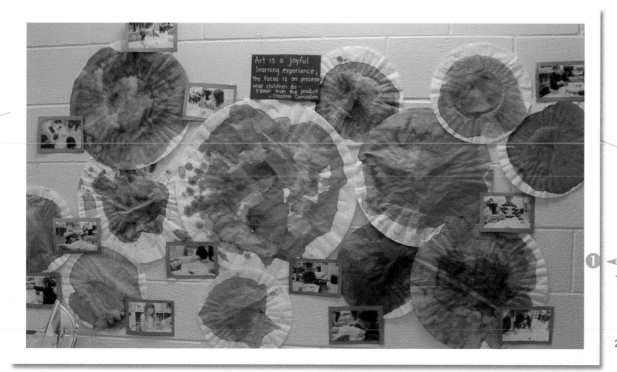

1. Children's colorful artwork, artistically displayed, with children's pictures and explanations of their work

2. A beautiful three-dimensional display of children's artwork highlighted with soft lighting

Artwork created by children and adults adds color, texture, and beauty to early childhood classrooms. Draw the children's attention to these creations by displaying the art in attractive ways. Sometimes these displays of artwork inspire children to try new art techniques or the displays simply expose them to art created in different ways. Local artists such as potters, weavers, or architects can visit, demonstrate, and display their work. Interacting with artists helps children discover that artists are all around them—and that they can be artists, too.

Plants and flowers soften the space, clean the air, and create visual interest in early childhood classrooms. For instance, a large corn plant has an interesting structure, with leaves growing out of the large stalk. It is also a plant that is very easy to care for, surviving both flood and drought. Vines, ferns, succulents, and cacti, introduce unique shapes and textures into the classroom space.

1. A grouping of plants, including a corn plant

2. Draping fabric softens and lowers the ceiling.

3. Colored fabric with a design is paired with a sheer fabric in an attractive arrangement.

The Impact of Light

Where you place lights and the brightness or softness of the light in your classroom can create a sense of calm or can contribute to children feeling over-stimulated. Light can focus attention on special artwork or other materials or shine equally brightly throughout the classroom. Many early childhood programs have fluorescent ceiling tubes that provide intense, and often over-stimulating, light for young children. Olds (2000) has reported that fluorescent lights actually flash 120 times per second, which can have a negative effect on some children. Replacing fluorescent tubes with full-spectrum bulbs will provide some relief from the brightness and harshness of the fluorescent lighting. Another lighting alternative, depending on the type of bulb, is to replace switches with dimmers that let you control the amount of light during different activities and times of the day based on what is happening in the classroom.

Early childhood classrooms need a variety of light sources so you can adjust and change the levels of light. Natural light is a pleasant and changing light source throughout the day, providing clear views of color in the classroom and of the children's work, although it may be necessary to shade or filter sunlight at times when its glare or brightness interferes with work. Use lighting from floor lamps, clamp lights, strip lights, and table lamps to focus on specific activities, displays, and tasks. Energy efficient bulbs are now widely available for most lamps. These single light sources can also provide a way to use less ceiling lighting at certain times. For example, a sturdy floor lamp next to a comfy chair in the library area may supply just the right amount of light to "read" a new book or revisit an old favorite. During a resting time, turn off all overhead lights and use soft lamp lighting for a calm and pleasant environment for relaxing.

1. Soft lighting is soothing and relaxing.

2. A sound panel muffles noise.

Sounds Make a Difference

Loud sounds, soft sounds, happy sounds, too many sounds—the quality and quantity of sounds in a classroom can impact children's behavior. Sound helps children determine what is happening and where activities are occurring. Often, the amount and quality of sound determines whether or not a classroom is a pleasant place. Too much sound can be overwhelming to young children who have little control over the noise in their environment or who may be especially sensitive to auditory stimulation.

You can control the sound in your classroom by using certain materials in high noise areas. For example, a classroom with a tile floor and cement walls magnifies the sounds produced by children. The sounds children make and hear as they actively participate in meaningful activities—laughing or disagreeing—will bounce from wall to floor and back many times, increasing the noise level significantly. You can add area rugs, soft furniture, pillows, and sound panels to absorb these sounds and make your classroom a more pleasant place.

Much of the space in the classroom is above young children's heads, so sound can travel across the entire room and impact other activities that are far from the source of the noise. Use raised floor areas and lofts to minimize the impact of sound by varying the distance between the ceiling and the floor. Because children can be distracted by noise, break up the sound in your classroom by draping fabric from the ceiling, creating a raised block-building area, hanging decorative fabric or cloth on the wall, or setting up a climbing loft.

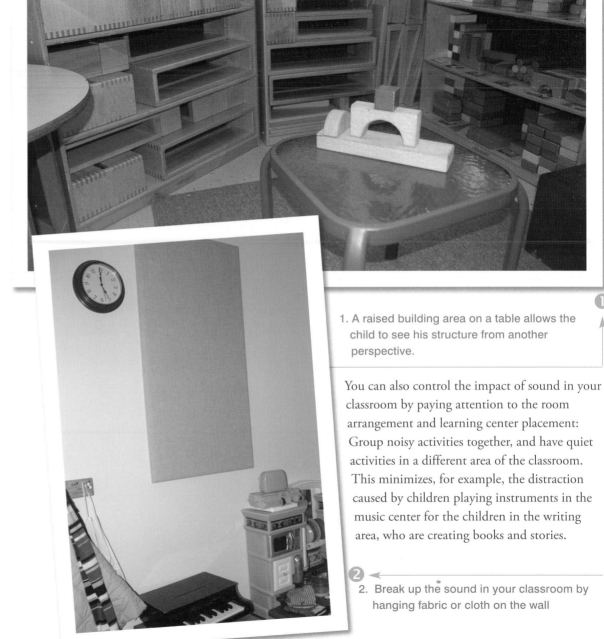

❶

1. A raised building area on a table allows the child to see his structure from another perspective.

You can also control the impact of sound in your classroom by paying attention to the room arrangement and learning center placement: Group noisy activities together, and have quiet activities in a different area of the classroom. This minimizes, for example, the distraction caused by children playing instruments in the music center for the children in the writing area, who are creating books and stories.

❷

2. Break up the sound in your classroom by hanging fabric or cloth on the wall

A Place for Everything, Everything in Its Place

Every day children engage in many different types of learning and activities. Young children have conversations, create projects, collaborate with others, and work independently. To accommodate children's learning and activities, the classroom should include a variety of spaces, such as a large area for community meetings, a place for reading, an art area, a blocks-and-construction area, and a space that facilitates work in small groups. The design of each space should encourage the learning and participation focus of that unique area.

Let the overall environment communicate to young children that this is a special place designed specifically for them. In this place they can explore, manipulate, move, and create as they develop competencies. Store and display classroom materials so that children understand what is available for their use and where to return items when they finish. Provide both consistency and change in your classroom—the basic design, placement, and expectations remain consistent, but materials, choices, and opportunities change over time. The furniture, materials, and display of materials impact the functionality of the classroom space. For instance, children's personal items will always be stored in their individual cubbies, but a new Restaurant Center may move into the classroom and remain for just three to four weeks. With this design, children know they always have a consistent, secure place for their personal treasures, but their interests are sparked by the new addition of a restaurant, which encourages socio-dramatic play with expanded language opportunities.

Olds recommends that the following six experiences be available to young children in their classrooms:

1. Quiet spaces: where young children can listen, be alone, or read
2. Structured activities: spaces where children can construct with blocks, manipulate small objects, and create artwork
3. Discovery materials: an area for children to explore natural materials, sand-and-water play opportunities, and a variety of art items or musical instruments
4. Dramatic play: centers for children, such as Home Living or Grocery Store, provide many materials to encourage dramatic play. Other opportunities include using puppets, creative drama, and other pretend play.
5. Large motor: where children may bounce or toss a variety of balls, explore climbers, rock in boats, open large books, and navigate obstacle courses
6. Therapeutic activities: places where children can relax on soft couches, snuggle soft toys and pillows, or can calm down in a private space

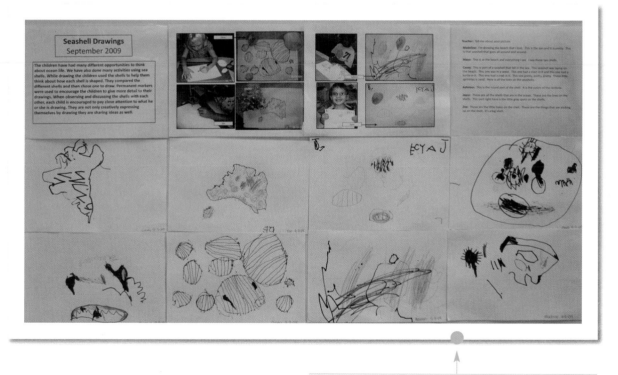

A place to display, share, store, and value children's work is an important classroom element.

To provide flexibility and variety in this small classroom the Home Living Center was transformed into a theater for a period of time.

A Secure and Supportive Environment

As the teacher, you are the person who has the most influence on both the physical and emotional environments of the classroom. A warm, caring, and responsive teacher communicates to young children that the classroom is a safe place where they are cared for in appropriate ways, that it is a place where they can be children and all their strengths and challenges will be respected. Communicate this warmth to children by greeting them when they arrive, listening to them when they have something to say, and providing choices that allow them to follow their interests. Show children that you value and respect each child's family and culture by displaying pictures of their families and by encouraging children and their families to share objects, songs, and stories from their cultures. This will foster their feelings of worth and make the classroom an inviting place.

In this secure and supportive environment, children can try new things without concern or fear, because their unique talents, capabilities, and challenges are

Flexibility is another characteristic of a well-functioning environment. Each classroom space, including its fixed features (walls, windows, and so on), is different. Each group of children who inhabits this space is unique. Each teacher and caregiver living in this place has special abilities and interests. Therefore, a critical element of design is the ability of the space, materials, and activities to change and adjust to match the people in the space. With careful planning, even a small space can be adjusted for children with different needs and diverse interests. For instance, it is possible to transform the Home Living Center into a Restaurant Center, Theater Center, or Fire Station for a period of three or four weeks. When the play or interest level of the children decreases, it is time to add a new material or to close the center. The Home Living Center can return to the space, and the changing center—restaurant or theater or fire station—can be boxed and stored away to use at a later time. Changing a center provides new opportunities for extending the play and learning for children, which is particularly important in a small classroom space.

Before

After

accepted. Changes, adaptations, and new opportunities allow each child to grow and feel confident. In this nurturing environment, children develop and expand their growing capabilities.

Some young children may feel overwhelmed by the sounds, movement, and visual stimulation of the groups of children and adults with whom they spend so much active time. In order to feel well nurtured, these children need a small cozy place where they can go to be quiet and relax. Providing this special area prevents major meltdowns, giving children the opportunity to regulate the amount of stimulation they receive and to recognize their need for quiet. A child can use a calming area when upset or frustrated

by events in the classroom; the child may choose to go to the place, or you may suggest that the child needs some quiet time. Either way, the child has the opportunity to self-regulate and determine when he or she is ready to re-enter the classroom activities. On pages 117–121 of this book is an example of a Calming Place in a PreK classroom.

A communication space lets children develop their problem-solving and communication skills, and adds to the positive emotional climate and nurturing environment of the classroom. Some classrooms call this space the Peace Center, as shown in the photos on this page. In the classroom depicted in the photo, the teacher spent time with the children helping them

learn about feelings and communicate caring thoughts to one another during the large-group meeting time. Lacking was a designated space for children to use when issues arose or time was needed to work through specific problems, feelings, and communication issues. The newly designed center offers children an opportunity to expand upon what they have learned about feelings through the use of the mirror, posters, and books. In addition, children can sit at the "peace" table to draw or write about problems, concerns, and possible solutions, keeping in mind what they have been learning about communicating caring messages to one another.

Valuing Diversity in the Classroom

Every child and adult in early childhood classrooms enters with a rich history of family, culture, traditions, and language that guides their interactions and preferences. This diversity provides enormous opportunities to explore differences and expand traditions by learning about those of others. It also provides challenges in negotiating differences, such as beliefs about expectations for child behavior, routines for meals and bed times, and family celebrations centered around holidays and birthdays. Valuing the diverse perspectives of each child and adult is critical for developing and supporting each individual's feelings of acceptance and self-confidence.

Early childhood classrooms support diversity with many different strategies, including:
- bringing culture into the classroom with displays of materials that are traditional for families,
- asking families to join classroom discussions and talk about a traditional food or family routines, or
- incorporating into classroom routines unique materials provided by families.

Plutro (2000) suggests the following specific ideas that respond to diversity, including:
- becoming conscious of personal biases and working to overcome them;
- learning the most important child-rearing values held by each family;
- supporting children's speech patterns and emergent language;
- structuring some classroom experiences and activities around materials contributed by parents;
- reflecting parents' occupations and talents in classrooms, on home visits, in community celebrations, and in other activities;
- avoiding a "holiday syndrome" or holiday-driven approach to curriculum; and
- developing some activities in which groups of children can focus on "alikeness" as well as difference.

> Diversity provides enormous opportunities to explore differences and expand traditions by learning about those of others.

Parent Contributions
Parents contributed beautiful fabric and decorations from India

Setting Up Appropriate Learning Environments

Young children between the ages of three and seven are moving along a developmental continuum, each child at his or her own pace. Knowing these developmental characteristics will help you determine the needs and interests of children in preschool and kindergarten; and this knowledge will influence how you set up an appropriate learning environment. Individual differences also impact the materials, activities, and experiences you select in a specific classroom. Careful observation and documentation of children's work, participation, and choices will help you identify these differences. Open-ended materials allow children at different stages of development to work side by side, learning from each other during the experience.

The following paragraphs provide general information about the typical areas of child development. It is important to recognize that these areas of development are interrelated. Children do not develop skills in isolation; rather, they strengthen their learning through activities that call upon multiple developmental areas.

Cognition: Young children are active learners who need hands-on experiences with real materials and objects, and opportunities to experiment. They are beginning to use symbols in their play. For instance, a block can represent a car, or a doll can be a baby sister. Children are very creative and need meaningful opportunities to develop problem-solving, thinking skills, and plans of action (Isbell, 2008). During this period, socio-dramatic play begins as children take on roles, collaborate, and learn to carry out a sustained sequence of events.

Help children learn about similarities as well as differences by inviting families to visit the classroom to share artifacts and stories representative of their cultures. For example, this photo is a temporary display of Japanese Origami dolls the children created after one of the children's mothers visited and shared information about Hinamatsuri or the Girls' Day celebration in Japan.

How does the environment support cognitive development?

- By providing natural materials and real objects that can be manipulated, actively explored, and used in many different ways;
- By setting up effective learning environments that provide a place for children to use symbols in their play. Open-ended and unique materials challenge young children to be flexible and fluent in their thinking.
- By displaying evidence of children's learning, which lets them revisit and treasure their work and see their development;
- By selecting materials for each space that match children's cognitive levels and challenge their thinking and creativity. For example, the Art Studio space typically includes large brushes and tempera paint. Adding several sets of watercolor paints, with small brushes or colored chalk, encourages new ways of thinking about art and artwork.

Language and Literacy Development: Young children are in a period of rapid language development. They are great collectors of new words and phrases, and are constantly asking about the meaning of language as they communicate, ask questions, and describe their experiences. They are interested in books and printed materials, and they are interested in "writing" and making meaningful marks to represent their ideas.

How does the environment support language and literacy development?

- By including writing materials such as pads, paper, pencils, markers, whiteboards, and clipboards in all centers to encourage drawing and writing;
- By including a large-group or community meeting area where children can listen to books, share their ideas, and make plans for the day;
- By including spaces for small-group experiences. Young children use more language and communicate more freely in small groups. Groups of three or four children are ideal to encourage children to talk and express their ideas and collaborate with others. Effective small groups can be created through the use of learning centers, creative projects, and group work.
- By including both traditional and new centers. Traditional centers, such as Blocks and Home Living, will inspire talking and discussion of the play activity. The introduction and use of new centers or collaborative projects will inspire children to use vocabulary that relates to the areas and materials.

This sign-up sheet, added to the Theater Center, provides an opportunity for developing literacy skills.

Social and Emotional Development: Early relationships are the foundation for children's future social and emotional development and success. Children who are between the ages of three and seven are developing self-confidence, skills for interacting with others, the ability to empathize and recognize their own and others' feelings, and the ability to use appropriate problem-solving strategies. In the classroom, children begin to learn the rules and expectations of this new social environment. Learning to wait for a turn to speak, to respect others' ideas, and to care for materials, are all important social and emotional skills that can be nurtured in an early childhood classroom. These skills require time and opportunities to develop and expand! In a classroom where a child feels loved and accepted by the teacher, he or she will be more willing to take risks and to venture to interact with others.

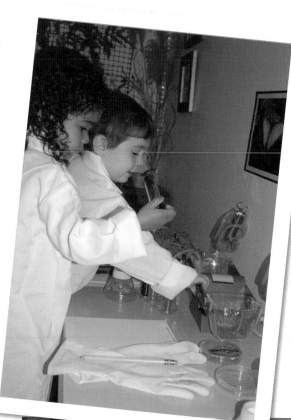

How does the environment support social and emotional development?

- By providing a sense of physical and emotional security. Eric Jensen, an expert in brain-compatible learning, has suggested that providing a sense of physical and emotional security is one of the most important aspects of the classroom environment.
- By having predictable routines to support this sense of security;
- By having group meetings to offer opportunities to discuss routines and classroom issues, and to support children's developing social interaction and conversation skills;
- By providing a wide variety of learning centers, which allows children to choose where and with whom they work. In these centers, children plan their play, assume roles, share materials, and communicate their thoughts, feelings, and expectations.
- By offering the opportunity for adults to observe as children play and interact. This observation time provides multiple teachable moments. For example, questions can support the development of problem-solving skills, or conversations can model and reinforce the appropriate expression of feelings and positive social interactions.

Children do not develop skills in isolation; rather, they strengthen their learning through activities that call upon multiple developmental areas.

Physical and Motor Development: Young children use their large motor skills to run, climb, throw, fall, and get back up. These large motor abilities are usually more developed than the small motor skills at this age, although this does vary from child to child. In the preschool years, children's still-developing small motor skills may interfere with their choice of activities and may produce frustration. For example, they may want to put multiple-piece puzzles together, but their hands just will not cooperate with their wishes.

How does the environment influence physical development?

- By providing many opportunities to develop and refine both large and small motor abilities, throughout the classroom as well as outdoors;
- By offering a range of materials, so children will be able to select items that match the level of their physical development and take advantage of opportunities for them to be successful. For instance, in the Writing Area, include different sizes of pencils, markers, and other tools for making marks. Paper of differing sizes, shapes, and textures provides additional choices and encourages different forms of writing, from scribbles to actual letters.

Motor Development
Cutting props for the theater production requires small motor skills.

Chapter 2

The Process of Planning
FOR SUCCESSFUL CHANGE

Creating the Vision

Whether you are planning to make a large or small change in an early childhood classroom, it is important to look at what is possible and at what you imagine would be ideal (what you dream). Combine these ideas with what you know about effective environments for young children. It is always helpful to involve others in thinking about changes in the classroom. You might ask another teacher, a principal, a university consultant, or parents to join you in thinking about the possibilities.

Many successful change processes begin with open-ended brainstorming about your dream classroom:

● Why would children and adults want to be in this classroom?
● What would this classroom look like and feel like?
● How do children and adults participate in this classroom?
● What would happen if this dream classroom became a reality?

In addition to brainstorming, your knowledge of young children and concrete information about your current environment provide critical information to guide the vision and planning process. One way to shape your vision is to determine how the children will experience the new, improved space. Lillian Katz (1999) described what she terms "a bottom-up perspective on quality." Using this approach, the

quality of the early childhood setting is determined by the way in which the learning and developmental needs of the children are being met.

There are also tools that provide information and data on classroom environments and interactions, such as the *Early Childhood Environment Rating Scale,* Revised, also known as ECERS-R (Harms et al, 2005); the Classroom Assessment Scoring System, known as CLASS, (Pianta et al, 2008); and the Early Language and Literacy Classroom Observation, also referred to as ELLCO, (Smith et al, 2008). ELLCO focuses specifically on the literacy environment. These tools provide insight into the strengths and opportunities for change in your environment by asking you to consider such things as physical features, types of interactions, classroom materials, and literacy materials.

Review both your dreams and the specific information you have collected to create a plan for what you want to change. Evaluate the possibilities, including the time and resources available, structural features that may both limit and provide opportunities, and the changes that will have the most profound impact for children.

Decluttering and organizing the storage area may be the first step in the design process. This will help you determine what you have, what could be used, and any additional materials that might be needed.

Decluttering and organizing
the storage area may be the first step
in the design process.

This area is underutilized. What could be moved to this area that would make better use of the space? This quiet corner might be a great place for an interesting library area.

Developing a Plan

As you move through the process of creating and enhancing environments and determining the changes, additions, and materials that are needed, it is important to keep your focus on the children and what they are doing in this environment. This will be the best indicator of the effectiveness of your environment for young children.

- Observe the children as they move through the day.
- Determine areas of the classroom that are working well and those that are not.
- Notice where children do not seem to know what to do or how to find the materials they would like to use.
- Watch whether the children are engaged in activities or are flitting from place to place. These observations will help you decide where you might begin and the spaces that need the most attention.

Take pictures of the classroom or the specific space you are contemplating changing. These pictures will give you a clear view of the arrangement of space and materials. When you live in a classroom and add materials to it, you become used to these additions because they happen gradually and over a period of time. Review the existing furniture and items that you have in the classroom and things that are in storage that can be used as you change the space. For example, a bookcase in storage can become a boundary for the new area, helping children determine where this space begins and ends. A low table can become a place to display some of the creations developed in this area.

This framed collage includes photos important to the teacher and a description of the training she received to work with young children. It is displayed at the entrance to the classroom and helps parents learn more about the person who is working with their children.

Review the elements of design on pages 9–19 to be sure that the change you envision, or the new space you want to create, is visually appealing, with beautiful accessories and a comfortable level of sound. Be sure that it will function as you intend, supporting the learning that you want to take place. Draw a rough sketch of your plan that includes the fixed features you cannot change and the locations of furniture and materials that can be moved. This sketch will provide a way to play with the arrangement and to try out different possibilities. Moving on paper is far easier than physically rearranging heavy items many times. But, even after carefully drawing the layout, you may still need to make adjustments when things are in place.

The following questions can help you think about your classroom and consider possibilities to create a beautiful and effective environment for teachers and children. It can also help you assess the progress toward your desired environment as you engage in the process of change. (The following questions appear in a checklist format on page 151.)

- When a child enters your classroom, does he or she see a warm and inviting place?
- Does every child see pictures that are attractively displayed and that reflect all the children who live in this community?
- What are the sounds the child hears when he or she is in the space?
- Do the classroom environment and materials demonstrate what is valued in this place?
- Are examples of each child's work and pictures of their involvement displayed so they can be admired by the children, parents, teachers, and other adults?
- Are a variety of areas available: quiet, active, messy, and large or small group? Can the children easily see where these areas are located?
- Are materials grouped together and close to where they will be used, nurturing children's independence?
- Are the materials and the space clearly organized so children can easily select the items that they need in their work?
- Are open-ended materials included to challenge children's creative thinking?
- Is there a place for children to pause, to be calm, and to reflect?
- Are beautiful items and natural materials displayed to be enjoyed?
- Is there a place to store the teacher's personal items?
- Are there places to sit comfortably?
- Is it possible to identify the special adults and their interests in this space by their personal displays?
- Is the lighting varied and controllable in the space that is being changed or in the new space being planned?
- Does this new feature or classroom area function effectively with the other components of the classroom?
- Does the environment provide opportunities for children and adults to "play" with learning and to explore, reflect on, and share learning experiences?

Introducing a New Feature

Creating new features in your classroom is exciting for both you and the children. Your thoughtful planning, materials selection, and implementation will help this addition to be successful and inspiring in your classroom.

It is essential that you prepare the children for the new feature in the classroom before they begin using the area. This preparation will help the children know how things work, what the possibilities are for activities, and how to work together in this new space or with this new feature in the classroom. This is the ideal time to introduce new vocabulary, explain materials, and establish procedures. Consider the following ideas for successfully introducing classroom makeovers to the children.

- Have a "grand opening" for the newly renovated space or new feature. Take the group to see the exciting new area they have been watching develop.
- Discuss the materials in the area using the appropriate names with explanations of how things might be used. Give several possibilities so the children understand that there are many different ways to use some items. Open-ended materials encourage creative thinking and problem solving.
- Help the children learn how to care for the materials and how to return materials to their proper places so the children become responsible members of the classroom community.

This display is a special new feature that makes the classroom environment more culturally sensitive to the children who live in this community.

- In community time, introduce the new logo or pictures of the new area, so children will be able to identify the area or center.
- Be prepared that many children will want to go to this new area on the first day. So, have a notebook or pad where you record the children who did not get to go. On the next day, refer to your list to show that their waiting is valued. Check to make sure every child has the opportunity to go to the new area during the first week or so.
- Take digital pictures of the children using the materials and participating in projects in the area. These can be displayed to inspire others' activities.
- Observe the use of the renovated space. How is it working? Do you have enough materials, or are there too many of some things? Is the placement of the furniture or props supporting the children's play?
- Sometimes it is necessary to enter the children's play in the new space. You can stimulate ideas, demonstrate possibilities, and encourage cooperation. But, take a minor role and get out of the play as soon as possible.
- Encourage cleanup by assisting the children, modeling methods, and commenting on the children's efforts.
- After center time is over, bring the children back to the large-group area. Talk with them about their participation in the area or new space. Write down their comments and post these in the center or area. Reflection is important to nurture learning and helps demonstrate the value of the children's work.

Enjoy the excitement of adding new possibilities for the children in your classroom. Recognize that you are expanding their learning opportunities. The true measure of the success of the environment is how it meets children's needs and how it nurtures the development of qualities that support positive attitudes, habits, and values to promote lifelong learning.

Chapter 3

Low-Cost,
BIG-IMPACT CHANGES

Getting Rid of the Clutter

Early childhood teachers are great collectors of materials: "You never know when I might need this." After a few years of collecting, classrooms can become filled with "stuff." Young children, who are often very visual, can be overstimulated by all of the materials in a classroom. Decluttering the classroom space can have a tremendous impact on the appearance of the area, how it functions, and what children do there. Decluttering is the essential first step in the process of creating a new feature or area in the classroom. If an item has not been used in the last three years, it is probably not going to be used. Donate these things to another program, or simply throw them away. You may be astonished by what decluttering can accomplish. The space is more open; things are easier to find; and children can be more focused on their activities. Many of the Real Classroom Makeovers on pages 43–121 include examples of decluttering to prepare for new spaces or features. Photos below also show how materials were minimized and storage covered to create a less distracting area.

Before

Decluttering is the first step in the process of creating a new feature or area in the classroom.

After

Small Changes

In an early childhood classroom, there are many different areas, numerous materials, and many possible arrangements of the furniture. Sometimes evaluating the entire classroom and determining where to begin can be overwhelming. It is easier to identify a specific area of the classroom or a particular problem to address than it is to redesign the whole space. For instance, you may recognize that the children cannot find materials in the art area without your assistance. Solving this problem may be as simple as regrouping the materials and displaying them in a way that provides visibility and accessibility for the children. Moving materials and improving storage can make a big change in the way children use the materials and return them to their place. The only cost for this easy change is the purchase of clear containers or attractive baskets.

Many low-cost changes have a tremendous impact on the classroom environment. For example:
- Use fabric to soften a space, identify an activity, or display a beautiful design.
- Use fabric to re-cover a tired couch or make comfy cushions that feel good to the touch.
- Drape fabric over an area to communicate that this is a special place to read or listen to stories.

Before

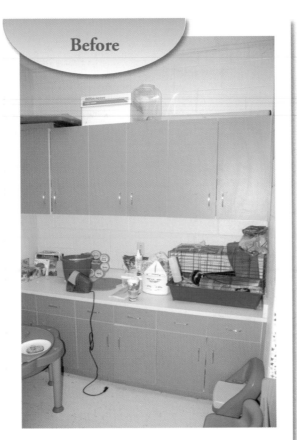

After

1. These plain but brightly colored cabinets are useful for storage but are not visually attractive.

2. Now, the cabinets are a place to display children's artwork, creating a gallery for their work.

The pictures on this page show how a teacher removed the doors from a large cabinet, added soft cushions, and created inviting spaces for reading or listening to music. These small projects can be done with inexpensive fabric remnants purchased at a discount store.

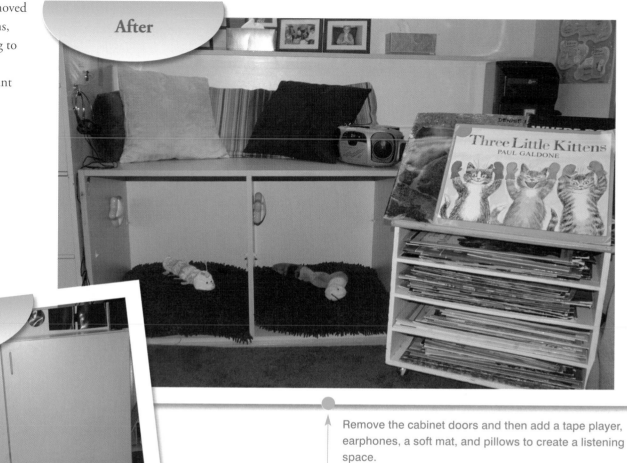

After

Before

Remove the cabinet doors and then add a tape player, earphones, a soft mat, and pillows to create a listening space.

Teacher's Space

You need a secure place in the classroom to keep your personal items. This place could be anything from a drawer in a closed cabinet to a small desk. But, how much usable space is needed for teachers' things?

Before

Teacher space is transformed into children's space.

Examine your classroom. How much of the classroom space is used by a teacher desk, file cabinets, storage cabinets, and teacher-only work stations? Making time to clean teacher space and remove items not needed in the learning environment often leads to a decluttered environment with more space for children's learning. In the kindergarten classroom shown on page 32, the teacher space is transformed into a comfortable area that invites children to read. In the sorting process, the teacher created two categories: items that will be organized and will remain in the classroom, and items that will be discarded. Because many early childhood teachers have a difficult time throwing things away, it is helpful to think of ways to distribute surplus materials to other early childhood programs that have few materials to use with their children. The teacher selected the resources she wanted to keep, organized them, and then placed them in a bookcase covered with fabric or a bamboo shade so the materials are no longer a distraction for the children but are easy for her to find.

After

The teacher selected the resources she wanted to keep, organized them, and then placed them in a bookcase covered with fabric or a bamboo shade so the materials are no longer a distraction for the children but they are easy for her to find.

Chapter 4

Building
A SENSE OF COMMUNITY
IN THE CLASSROOM

Each classroom community includes the children, teachers, other adults, and families. As Jim Greenman expresses in his book *Caring Spaces, Learning Places,* a sense of community is the feeling of caring and learning as both personal and professional relationships grow, are respected, and are sustained over time with common goals and interests. In such a classroom, people learn from each other and support each other throughout the day and year. Young children feel a part of this community and adults appreciate both the other adults and the children who share this space. In a classroom community, children have a sense of belonging and acceptance.

How does the classroom environment create a sense of belonging and acceptance?

Create a welcoming environment at the entrance with plants, a bench, and pillows.

After

Before

After

Our Community

Kendall Aiden Riley Bethany Haley Tanner Alexis Chase Storm Jos

Now, pictures of all the children in the classroom are displayed with an additional collection of photos showing them involved in classroom activities.

Creating a welcoming and inviting entrance is the place to begin. As the old saying goes, you only have one chance to make a good first impression. The same idea applies when entering a classroom: The entrance either welcomes you in and is personalized for those who live and work within, or it is cold and uninviting. Which would you choose to enter? (See Chapter 5, the "Welcome Area" section on pages 111–116, for more details.)

Developing a sense of place connects the classroom to its surroundings. For example, the inspiration for creating a sense of place can be right outside the building. The view outside the kindergarten classroom window in the photo below is a beautiful field and mountain ridge. This teacher brings the sense of nature from the outside into the classroom by using natural

hues on the walls, by using wood shelves and tables, and by highlighting the theme of nature and the outdoors in the learning centers and classroom experiences. Connecting the classroom to its surroundings helps create a classroom connection to the entire surrounding community.

Valuing each member of the community, which includes children, teachers, parents, and other adults, is another way of creating a sense of belonging and acceptance. The children are the focus of the classroom community, which values their unique interests, talents, and choices. Showing and treasuring children's work and displaying photos of each child in the classroom communicates that this classroom space is designed specifically for them.

Teachers are also members of this community; they plan, design, and support young children's development. Each teacher has personal interests, varied experiences, and possessions that can be added to the classroom environment to communicate who she is. For instance, a teacher may bring a blanket that she knitted for the chair she uses during circle time. The blanket invites conversation about her interest in knitting, and it adds a personal touch to this space. In addition, a display of pictures of the teacher, her family, her pets, and her interests helps other members of the community recognize how the teacher is special.

Each teacher has personal interests, varied experiences, and possessions that can be added to the classroom environment to communicate who she is.

Adding items that are personally meaningful to the teacher makes the space unique. This teacher is also a drummer, so the display, which includes a hut, several drums, and pictures, helps the children learn about his interests.

Parents and grandparents are valued members of the community and are often invited into the classroom. They enrich the classroom community's understanding and knowledge about the children, their families, and their cultures. Parents and grandparents build a sense of community by participating in activities in the classroom, cooking with the children, sharing music and stories from their cultures, and helping you create an environment that is sensitive to the children and their families. Demonstrate that each family is special and respected by displaying family photos in the home living area or other classroom areas.

Early childhood classrooms are often located in schools, centers, or churches where there are many interesting people who can enrich the classroom by visiting, sharing their stories, and building relationships with the children. These experiences will expand the children's world and help them develop an appreciation for the diversity of the people who care about them. For example, children enjoy and are enriched by visits and interactions with staff: consider inviting the janitor, the housekeeper, or the cook.

Having effective group time means providing an inviting and attractive place for group meetings. Where you and the children gather should support the sense that you are a community of learners. The location of this gathering place is very important because it will use a significant portion of the classroom space. Teachers often find that placing the large-group area next to a wall or in a corner cuts down on distractions and helps children focus their attention. However, if this place contains blocks or manipulatives on open shelves that are easy to reach, young children will be drawn to these materials. Instead of listening to the story, they will be stacking blocks or pulling a game off the shelf. Young children, who are very visual, will also be distracted if there is too much "stuff" in this area. Some materials may be needed during certain portions of group time, such as during discussions of the calendar or the weather. But, if these charts are on display all the time, they can be distracting as well.

During group time:

- You might talk with the children about the plans for the day. Consider encouraging the children to share and discuss their ideas, feelings, and plans.
- You and the children might listen and respond as different individuals share their ideas about a wonderful book, discuss the content, relate the book to the real world, and point out a moral of the story that might apply to the classroom environment.
- You and the children might actively participate in group time by singing new songs as well as the group's favorites.
- You might engage the children's critical thinking by discussing ideas for center time and work-choice possibilities. After center time, children can return to this area to reflect on their play and projects.
- The group can meet in this area when they are welcoming a visitor or preparing for lunch.
- At the end of the day, a closing group provides time to reflect on the day, discuss activities for the next day, and have a closing routine.

A consistent pattern and sequence for this group meeting time (for example, singing a welcome song; greeting the children; discussing a theme, unit, or project; identifying the centers that are open; describing a new center or new materials in a center; selection of centers by the children; and, finally, a transition song, such as, "This Is the Way We Go to Centers") gives children a sense of security because they know what to expect, how things will progress, and how things will end. Within that sequence details may vary—topics change, new materials are added—providing the excitement that novelty brings and giving group time elements of predictability as well as variations that invite interest. The "Gathering Place" Real Classroom Makeover on pages 106–110 provides details about one classroom's experience of creating a new space for group meetings.

Learning about and practicing responsibility in the classroom helps children develop a sense of ownership and pride. Children use the space to work, play, and learn together. There are many ways to remind children of their classroom job responsibilities. In the photo below, the teacher has labeled individual pockets with a picture and words to represent the job. Children choose the job they wish to be responsible for and put their name stick in that pocket. Change the jobs daily or weekly.

1. Using pictures and words on these containers enhances the sense that "I belong in this place."

2. Mail pouches labeled with photos of the children.

Identifying children's personal spaces supports a sense of belonging. Classrooms contain many areas that are shared by all the members of the community. Adding specific places for individual children is another strategy to support each child's identity within the community and also to provide functional areas that support each child's work and interactions in the classroom. Using pictures and words enhances the sense that "I belong in this place." For example, because many children in PreK and kindergarten classrooms do not read print, it is important to provide labels that use both photos and printed names. In the photo on this page, the teacher labels mail pouches (a clear shoe holder) with photos of the children, which inspire children to write or draw and send messages to one another using the mail pouches.

The photos on the next page show another classroom where the teacher provides individual spaces to store and display work to demonstrate the value of children's work. In early childhood classrooms, the focus is on the *process* of learning, which means that work is ongoing. For this reason, a project needs to be stored where it can be accessed, worked on, stored, and then accessed again. Clearly defined storage offers children the opportunity to be responsible for their own learning. For example, label clear stacking storage boxes for each child to store his or her work, or provide a basket for storing draft writing books that children can obtain and return independently.

Providing choices for individual work contributes to a sense of community. When children have the opportunity to make choices that let them select their own activities and follow specific interests, they become more engaged and persistent in their work. Having times when children can make their own choices gives them some control of their day. For example, in some early childhood classrooms, children are able to choose any center they would like to work in and to remain in that area until they have completed their involvement. One example of providing individual work choices, as depicted on this display board (see the photo on the upper left), uses icons to represent work areas or centers. In this photo, the children have a few "must do" work assignments or centers, and then have five other activities or centers to choose from once the "must do" work is complete. Curriculum and learning plans for the children determine the work assignments and the areas available.

Working in small groups brings children together to share ideas, work collaboratively on projects and activities, and learn from one another. When designing the environment, create spaces where small groups can work together. Incorporating small tables into center areas provides multiple spaces for small groups to work and play together and helps build a sense of community in the classroom.

Chapter 5

Real
CLASSROOM
MAKEOVERS

The Importance of Play

Play is a major avenue for learning in the preschool and early elementary years. Many young children, however, have little experience playing and exhibit immature play skills when they enter early childhood programs. A quality environment provides enriched opportunities for play so that young children can fully experience the learning benefits possible as they touch, feel, experiment, and create.

Learning centers are an effective way to organize the classroom space to encourage play through participation in small groups (Isbell, 2008). When children play in small groups they have more opportunities to use language, influence the activity, and share ideas. In these groups, fewer disagreements and conflicts occur since only three to four children are involved in the play. Therefore, this size group provides a safe place for children to develop skills, expand language, and practice working with peers.

When children are mature players, they begin to participate in socio-dramatic play, creating a sequence of events, taking on roles, engaging in collaboration, and becoming immersed in their play for long periods of time (Smilansky & Shefatya,1990). Learning centers, where materials are organized around a theme, encourage the development of this form of play. For example, Home Living, a traditional center, provides the space and materials for children to take on the

roles of different family members, and often includes a kitchen where children can prepare dinner. When children play in centers such as the Home Living Center, they choose roles, use language related to the center, and focus on the sequence of events they create.

It is important for children to choose where they would like to go and to plan what they will do in the learning center. When children follow their interests, their play is more sustained and engaging. An important step towards using centers effectively is to provide time for the children to reflect on their play. This discussion can include posing questions about what children did in the center, what they created, and whether or not they want to return to that play scenario tomorrow.

Inspire sustained and engaging center play with the following ideas:
- Provide centers (themes) that will extend and enrich the play, such as centers that encourage socio-dramatic play and role-taking. These might include restaurant, camping, or doctor's office.
- Provide sufficient time for in-depth play to occur. (This will vary in different groups of children, but 40–60 minutes is often suggested.)
- Select materials, props, and toys that support the theme and children's play.
- Help children plan their play and reflect on it when center time is concluded.
- Coach children who need help engaging in play or pair them with more mature players.
- Observe and record the children's play and specific happenings to improve the play environment.

Play is a learning activity that should be nurtured in early childhood classrooms. Learning centers provide places, props, and peers so this development can occur (Bodrova & Leong, 2007).

> When children follow their interests, their play is more sustained and engaging. An important step toward using centers effectively is to provide time for the children to reflect on their play.

Real Classroom Makeovers Support Children's Play

The Real Classroom Makeovers in this chapter provide concrete examples of how to apply your knowledge of environments, early learning, and child development to create and enhance learning centers that provide optimal opportunities for young children.

To create this book, the authors recruited preschool, PreK, and kindergarten teachers interested in participating in the project. These teachers collaborated in planning the specific renovations for their spaces and worked with the authors to implement the plans in their classrooms. In each of the makeovers, you will read about the teacher's thoughts and plan of action, see before and after photos, and learn about some of the specific details of the makeovers. The goal of each makeover is to enhance the beauty of the space and to improve the learning that takes place in the space. Both the creativity of the participants and the results are amazing. The changes range from very simple rearrangements and additions to large, but still easy, construction projects. Use your imagination to think about how some of these ideas might work in your classroom as you consider how you might enhance the environment for all children and adults who "live" in the space.

The Real Classroom Makeovers in this chapter are divided into groups based on the primary focus of the makeover. Each center is designed to integrate opportunities for literacy and language development through enriched materials that encourage more language and literacy acts, such as pretend reading, writing, and printing (Morrow, 1990; Neuman & Roskos, 1992; Vukelich, 1991). Equipping all learning centers with a variety of literacy tools increases the number of experiences and opportunities for reading and writing. Some items to consider adding to learning centers include paper; pens or pencils; markers; books; notebooks; and authentic writing materials representative of the center, such as menus, recipe cards, and notepads. Arranging high-impact literacy centers, such as writing, listening, computers, and library centers, together offers children opportunities to enhance and develop literacy skills as they work in a variety of centers integrating reading, writing, and oral language.

Library Canopy

Before

Developing a Vision

Why do you want to redo this area of the classroom?

The library center is the most important center in the room. I would like the center to be multi-purpose. I would like to add writing, puppets, or other materials.

What learning would you like to take place in this part of your classroom?

I would like to promote oral language development, peer interactions, and playing at reading.

What is working that you would like to keep?

The area is organized so the children can put books back on the shelf. The center has natural light, so sometimes we don't need the fluorescent lights.

What are your concerns?

There are several children in the classroom with special needs ranging from language delays to autism. Care must be taken so the changes are not visually overwhelming for these children. Soft lighting would be calming too. To address these sensitivities, changes will need to be made gradually with the introduction of only one or two new items or visuals at a time.

Description of the Classroom

This is a large classroom with an open design. Huge windows, above a ledge that displays a few plants, line an entire wall of the classroom. For a portion of the day, fluorescent lights are not necessary, so only natural light is used. There are 23 kindergarten children with a teacher and an aide in the class. More than 10 of the children in this classroom have Individual Education Plans (IEPs), identifying the need for classroom adaptations. The floor is tiled and is covered with two large area rugs. One of these rugs is located in the library area, where there are a number of big books on a rack and a collection of children's books displayed on a wooden unit.

Plan of Action

- Place a fabric drape in a neutral color over a portion of the library area, producing a cozy and inviting area for reading that is not being overly visually stimulating.
- Select and purchase eight yards of neutral fabric; check out discount fabric stores.
- Consider moving books, puppets, stuffed animals, and other materials in the classroom to the library area.
- Evaluate the condition of the rug currently in the area.
- At a later point, add flashlights and/or lanterns.

After

The bamboo shade provides an interesting background for the unique owls the children designed to be displayed in the area. The tree-stump stools add to the natural feel of the space. The floor lamp, with three shades, allows light to be focused on reading in the area.

Center Drawing: Library Canopy

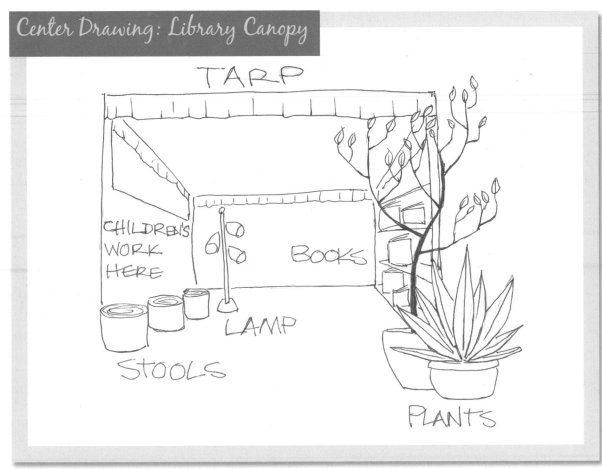

Teacher's Comments

- My students are begging to go in the library. Sometimes I will look over and a few of them are trying to sneak in. Sneak into the Library Center, can you imagine?
- Adults have commented that my room is "cozier" and more "inviting." The children were so excited as they walked into the classroom today.

Children's Comments

- Some comments were "Whoa!" One little boy asked, "What is that?" I told him it was a canopy. Then he met every student coming in and said, "Look we have a new canopy in our library."
- Others said, "We have a new library"; "It's beautiful"; "I really like the classroom!" "Can I go in there?"

Special Feature

Place a large canopy or curtain over a portion of the library area. This addition produces an interesting place to read, relax, or regroup. The neutral upholstery fabric is brown and soft. It is attached to the bottom of the two windows with industrial strength Velcro®, to support the weight of the fabric. The other end of the fabric is stapled to a wooden curtain rod, which is used to hold the length of the fabric.

Materials to Add

bamboo shades

baskets to hold puppets and books

books collected from around the room

floor lamp

several flashlights

wooden dowel rod, 1" in diameter

wooden tree stumps (3)

8 yards of upholstery fabric

Library Tent

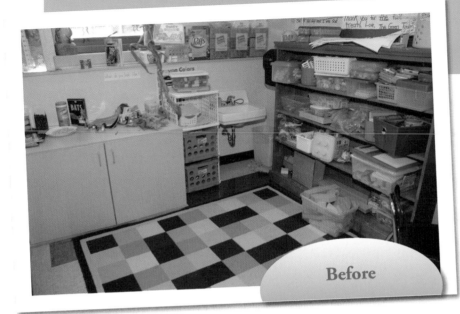

Before

Developing a Vision

Why do you want to redo this area of the classroom?

The current space is not inviting. I want to have more literacy connections in the library such as listening and/or writing. I want the Library Center to be the focus of the room.

What learning would you like to take place in this part of your classroom?

I would like more opportunities for the children to develop literacy and to learn from working in small groups.

What is working that you would like to keep?

The centers and small groups are in good locations in the classroom.

What are your concerns?

The area needs more defined boundaries. I would like the center to be more interesting, vibrant, and inviting. Currently, the library is located by the main door and entrance into the classroom, which produces many distractions as the children enter and exit the space. Library materials are located throughout the classroom.

Description of the Classroom

This classroom is located in an older building that has received some renovations since it was built in 1930s. These changes include air-conditioning, lights, and shades for the wall of windows in the space. The floor is tile with an area rug in one location. There are many literacy materials located all over the classroom. More than 20 kindergarten children and a teacher use this space. The Library Center does not have a focal point or special feature to entice the children to go to the center.

Plan of Action

- Move the location of the Library Center away from the door.
- Collect all literacy materials located throughout the classroom.
- Cover the back of a large bookcase that will be facing the community/circle area so that it will be more attractive and will provide another place to display children's work.
- Focus on a nature theme for the area, and decide what special addition might inspire children to go to the area and remain for longer periods of time.
- Find items that will support this theme, such as flashlights, lanterns, and other camping items.
- Select featured books that match the theme and draw the children to "read."

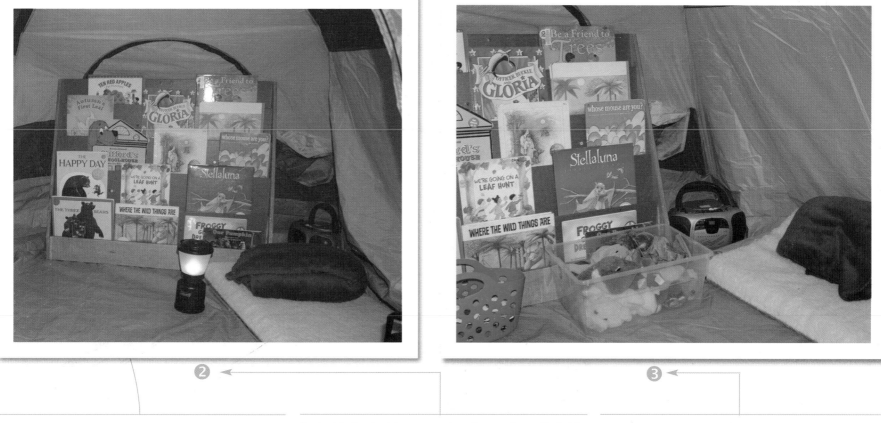

2

3

1. A string of lights and an artificial tree create an outdoor feel

2. Inside the tent is a cozy place for reading with light from the lantern. The pillows, stuffed toys, and a blanket make this a soft, inviting area.

3. The tape player gives children the choice of listening to a story.

Center Drawing: Library Tent

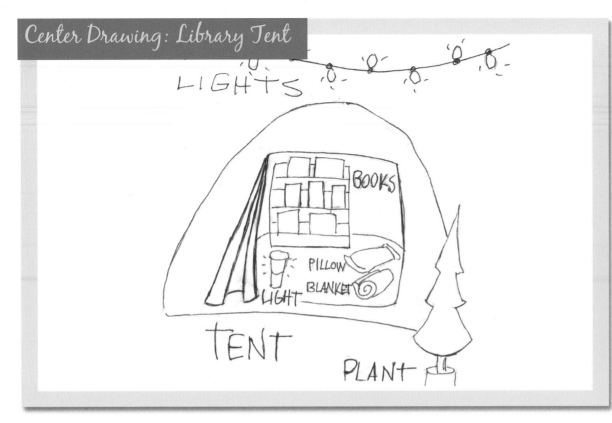

Special Feature

An outdoor tent set up in the Library Center creates a defined place for enjoying books. The book display rack and other literacy materials are inside this tent, which is large enough to contain a tape player and tapes for listening. To set the mood, place other items, such as flashlights, a battery-operated lantern, soft pillows, stuffed animals (to add a cozy feel), and a fleece blanket, inside the tent.

Materials to Add

small outdoor tent (available at discount stores for under $50)

clothesline and a string of twinkling lights (suspend over the center for a special effect)

several large, soft pillows colored brown, tan, or green

2 LED flashlights (batteries have a long life)

outdoor lantern that is small and not too bright

soft throw or small blanket, which softens the area and may be used to lie on while reading

tape or CD player and stories on cassettes or CDs

Teacher's Comments

- I love that the space is so open. It allows more options to be placed in the area.
- The size of the tent provides adequate space for several students to relax and enjoy a book.
- Since the renovations in the Library Center, I have noticed that the students are more engaged in the materials. Before it was revamped, students were wandering around the room or playing with puppets instead of reading in the area. Now I can't get them to come out.
- Several students who used to moan and complain when it was their time to go to library now beg to go there. They were so excited about the new setup and being able to go the library campsite. They also liked the listening station being included, as it provided another option in the tent.
- The new Library Center is definitely an asset to our classroom.

Children's Comments

- Wow, this is cool!
- One child who had already been to the library that morning asked, "When can I go to the library again? Can I go to the library instead of the computer?"

Before: Writing Center

Literacy Area

Developing a Vision

Why do you want to redo this area of the classroom?

Computers are in two different areas of the room. One group is located in a loud part of the classroom. The listening area is too small and is located by the busy entrance door. It requires teacher assistance. The writing area is too close to the entry, and it is not connected to other literacy areas and books. Children enjoy writing on the whiteboard, so it makes sense to move the writing area near the larger whiteboard in the room.

What learning would you like to take place in this part of your classroom?

Children need multiple literacy experiences that include opportunities to read, write, listen, and to engage in activities that enhance oral language, phonological awareness, print awareness, alphabetic knowledge, vocabulary, and comprehension. Increasing independence, confidence, and competence in writing and computer skills are goals for all learners.

What is working that you would like to keep?

Many of the materials work well; they just need to be better placed for functionality.

What are your concerns?

Electricity and Internet connections are necessary, unless wireless and battery-powered devices such as mp3 players or iPods are available.

Before: Listening Center

Before: Computer Center

Before: Book Display

Before: Learning Center

Description of the Classroom

This classroom is located in a building that was built in 1971 and opened in 1972. Furniture was purchased to use as cubbies because there is not a built-in coatroom. These cubbies consumed valuable space in the classroom, so they were moved to the entrance area. This one change allowed us to create a large literacy area. Initially, computers, listening devices, and books were spread around the room in small and undefined spaces. Books were located on a freestanding shelf in the middle of the room, along with other materials, such as games and puzzles. There are no windows in this PreK space. Bathrooms and sinks are located outside the space. There are 20 children, a teacher, and an aide in this classroom.

Plan of Action

- Move computers, listening, and writing centers to a central location to create a literacy area made up of smaller literacy centers.
- Incorporate a variety of literacy experiences that reflect different learning modes—auditory, visual, and bodily kinesthetic experiences.
- Add a standing stamp table.
- Move the centers closer to the whiteboard.
- Add softness with floor pillows and fabric on bulletin boards.
- Add plants.
- Add a mailbox and personalized individual mailboxes.

After: Listening Area

After: Computer Center

After: Standing Letter-Stamping Table

After: Writing Center

After: Learning Center

After: listening area—Add softness with pillows, rugs, and beanbags, and homey elements with lamps and plants

After: computer area—Group computers to encourage collaboration; include books in the area.

After: book area—Include books throughout the room, as you see here in the listening, computer, and writing centers.

After: writing area—Pocket mailboxes encourage children to write to one another, and the mailbox encourages reading as children deliver letters to one another.

After: Standing Letter-Stamping Table—This bodily kinesthetic stamp center allows children to stand while stamping letters and words.

After

Special Features

The special features in this literacy space are the standing table and the personalized mailboxes. Young children like and need to move. Adding a standing table for the letter-stamping area allows children to move as they work. Using this recycled printer table as the main table for the letter-stamping area also provides built-in storage for the necessary supplies: paper, stamps, and stamp pads. Inexpensive clear shoe holders are used to create personalized mailboxes for the writing area. These simple and inexpensive features create interest and motivation for writing and communicating with others.

Materials to Add

computers

letter stamps

listening headsets, books on tape or CD

magnetic letters, letter-forming Wikki-Stix

mailbox and personalized mail pouches

plants (for a welcoming touch)

variety of books

variety of pens, pencils, crayons, markers

variety of writing surfaces—small whiteboards, chalk boards, Etch-A-Sketch, sand in a baking sheet, clipboards

whiteboard space for practice

Teacher's Comments

- Children really enjoy writing on the whiteboards.
- The space allows children to work individually while I work with a small group.
- All of the literacy areas— listening, computers, and writing—are together. Children can follow their interests from one area to the next.

Children's Comments

- Books are everywhere!
- I like using the wiki-sticks in writing to make words.
- I like writing my friends' names. I just look on the wall and see the names. Then I know how to write them.
- I liked listening to the stories while I was reading the books in listening.
- The stamps are fun because you can stamp your name or a friend's name and send them mail.
- I like reading books on the big pillows in listening. I like mailing letters to my friends. I made mail for Alex.

Construction

Developing a Vision

Before

Why did you want to redo this area of the classroom?

I would like to provide more items that are developmentally appropriate in my classroom. The block area could include math and literacy opportunities that would accompany and support the children's construction.

What learning would you like to take place in this part of your classroom?

I would like the center to promote spatial reasoning, problem solving, and math skills such as size, number, and pattern. The center might include books about building, which would encourage literacy development.

What is working that you would like to keep?

There are mats that the children can work on in the area. A number of outlets are easily accessible. Materials for the center are in tubs, which are easy for children to transport.

What are your concerns?

The center needs more materials and supplies that can be used in children's construction and investigations. I would like the center to be integrated with writing, literacy, and, possibly, social studies.

Description of the Classroom

This classroom is located in a school that was built in the 1930s. It has been renovated several times with the addition of air-conditioning, and other updates. This space houses 22 kindergarten children, more than 75 percent of whom receive free or reduced lunch.

Large windows with glare-reducing shades occupy one wall of the space. Two area rugs, one in the group meeting space and one in the block area, cover the tile floor. Large metal storage cabinets with doors are located on the back wall and in several locations around the classroom. There are outlets and strips used to power a television, computers, and lights. Most materials are organized and stored in plastic containers to be brought out for activities during the day.

Plan of Action

- Collect all the blocks and accessories for this center. Evaluate and determine what additional items to add to make this an effective area of the classroom.
- Review books, writing materials, and other literacy items in the classroom to integrate into the area.
- Explore ideas, such as pictures, drawings, and representations of buildings or other materials, to make the area more attractive and interesting, so the children will be drawn to the area and the materials found there.
- Use fabric, rugs, and sound-absorbing materials to reduce the noise of structures being knocked down or children playing with cars or trucks.
- Decide which blocks and/or accessories to display in the open bookcase and which to store in the closed cabinet.
- Create a chart that lists the learning that occurs when children are using blocks. The opportunities for learning will relate to the curriculum that is currently being used in this kindergarten.

❶

1. Display pictures of unique buildings to inspire children's creativity.

❷

2. Provide hard hats and goggles to encourage role playing.

❸

3. Offer an overhead projector with colored blocks to provide another way of building.

Center Drawing: Construction

CONSTRUCTION

Teacher's Comments

- The children are very interested in the new Block Center. They are excited about playing with the colored magnetic blocks and the rainbow blocks on the overhead projector. They especially like the colored blocks that project onto the wall.
- The children use color and shape words naturally to describe what they build.
- There have been no behavior problems in the new center because the children's engagement level is so high.

Children's Comments

- Wow, awesome!
- Hey, I can do everything, I can build a city on the wall, I can watch myself build my house, I made a barn, I built a school, It [the center] is so big, like our school.

Special Feature

An overhead projector found in storage was added to the block area. The projector was placed on a small children's desk that also provided an easily accessible space for storing blocks. Colored plastic blocks were purchased to project the color and shapes of the design on a fabric-covered wall. This new equipment entices children to explore the area and provides opportunities to experience a new way of looking at building. Paper and markers encourage drawing and symbolic representations of children's structures.

Materials to Add

books related to construction
new colored blocks
pictures of unusual buildings
plastic hard hats and goggles

scrap fabric to cover board
small multicultural wooden workers
soft area rug
writing materials: paper, markers, pencils

Blocks

Before

Developing a Vision

Why do you want to redo this area of the classroom?
I would like to have more literacy connections in the Block Center. The center is in need of a basic set of good blocks and additional types of blocks that encourage different building techniques. Currently there is a hodgepodge of materials that makes it difficult for children to find the items they need and return the materials to the appropriate place.

What learning would you like to take place in this part of your classroom?
I would like to promote oral language in the block area. We could also encourage literacy opportunities such as reading and writing. For example, a child might build a structure and then name it. We would also like the Block Center to support children's problem-solving skills.

What is working that you would like to keep?
The children have built a farm in the space, which accommodates four students.

What are your concerns?
We do not have a good variety of building blocks and we need more accessories, such as family figures, cars, trucks, and other props in the classroom/space. The space is small, and the area does not have boundaries that the children can easily understand.

Description of the Classroom

This kindergarten classroom is located in an older school building in an inner-city community. For many of these children, this is their first experience in an early childhood program. The space contains a large number of metal cabinets with doors. The cabinets are on the back wall of the classroom and in other places around the room. The walls are a light gray and the tile flooring is also light. There is a full wall of large windows that provide light and a view of an outdoor area. Bathrooms are down the hall from the classroom, with a water fountain outside the door. The space selected for blocks is small and has a row of computers behind it. There are a limited number of blocks and accessories in the classroom.

Plan of Action

- Determine the number, types, and sizes of blocks that are currently available in the classroom. Evaluate their usefulness.
- Purchase a rug that is attractive and will provide sound absorption.
- Order new blocks and accessories to expand the building and learning possibilities in this area.
- Determine a way to cover the storage area that is in the space but is not used by the children.
- Create a special feature to challenge the children to think, build, and problem solve in new ways. Examples of special features could include displaying a collection of animals that might engage the children's interest in creating a zoo, or displaying photographs of unusual structures to inspire children to build different types of buildings, such as skyscrapers, parking garages, or log cabins.
- Use clear containers that fit in the bookcases to hold blocks, accessories, and other materials.
- Have paper and markers in the area so the children can reflect on their building and draw pictures of their projects.
- Find a set of blueprints that the children can look at and use in the area, adding another literacy and design possibility.
- Make a chart to identify what children are learning in the block area.

1. A poster shows what children are learning in the block area.

2. Movable block storage has an unbreakable mirror on top to provide another perspective.

Center Drawing: Blocks

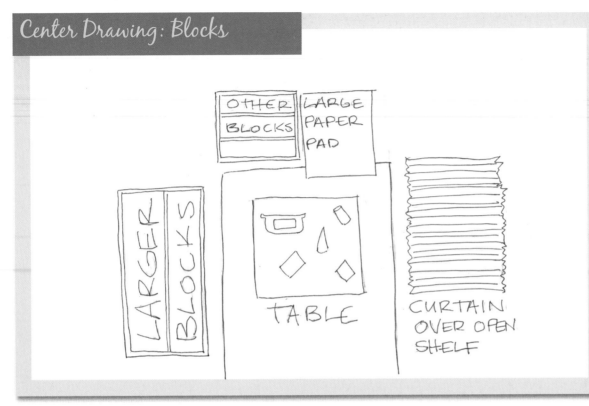

OTHER BLOCKS

LARGE PAPER PAD

LARGER BLOCKS

TABLE

CURTAIN OVER OPEN SHELF

Teacher's Comments

- The new Block Center and variety of materials really engages the children.
- I find the children making new structures and ramps, which increases their creative thinking and problem solving.
- The Block Center helps my students work cooperatively—and they actually do it pretty quietly.

Children's Comments

- I like the squishy blocks.
- All the cars are very awesome, and you can make lots of different designs.
- This is cool.
- I love going to this center.

Special Feature

A movable block cart created out of wood and plywood is designed for young children to use while standing. Blocks are stored on the shelf inside the unit. The cart rolls on canisters, so it can be moved easily into and out of the center as needed. The top is covered with an unbreakable mirror that allows the children to see their structures from many different perspectives. This new building site encourages the children to think about their structures and see them in different ways.

Materials to Add

5' x 7' area rug

charts

foam blocks

markers

people figures, including people with special needs

scraps of lumber, including longer pieces and unusual shapes

set of blueprints

trucks and cars

unbreakable mirror

wood, plywood, and tools (to construct movable block cart and mirror unit)

wooden blocks

Manipulatives

Developing a Vision

Why do you want to redo this area of the classroom?

Fine motor manipulatives are located in two separate areas of the classroom. The children do not see the materials as tools for constructing or creating. There is no space for children to play with the materials. They have to take the materials to other parts of the room and don't seem to use them, due to the lack of space available for construction.

What learning would you like to take place in this part of your classroom?

Fine motor manipulatives provide opportunities for children to explore, construct, and create. Children learn concepts such as sorting, classifying, counting, and learning about objects in motion. They also develop fine motor control.

What is working that you would like to keep?

Clear containers that are used to house materials work well for children to see what is available and where to return materials once their play is finished.

Before

What are your concerns?

The quantity of materials and space—there are many materials and not enough space to use the materials.

Description of the Classroom

This classroom is located in a building which was built in 1971 and opened in 1972. There are no windows. There is fixed row of cabinets with a counter on one side of the room. The floor is tile. A large area rug is used for the gathering space, and a few smaller area rugs are used throughout the room. Fine motor manipulatives are located in two different areas in the classroom; neither area is defined as a fine motor manipulatives center. The shelf used for the new manipulative center is attached to the wall and is immovable. The class is a state-funded PreK with 20 children, a teacher, and an aide.

Plan of Action

- Place all the fine motor manipulatives in one area to create a center.
- Organize the fine motor manipulatives so they are more accessible and inviting.
- Offer a choice of work space—both tabletop and floor space.
- Reduce the number of materials.
- To avoid distraction, cover the materials you do not want children to use.

Before

Before

After

1. Although the manipulatives bins were organized well in clear containers, they were located on opposite sides of the room. They were not used often due to lack of play space.

2. Easy-to-carry, labeled baskets make play and cleanup simple for the children.

Before

After

books about shapes, building, and other topics related to structures being created, such as *Architecture Shapes* by Michael J. Crosbie, *Museum Shapes* by The Metropolitan Museum of Art, *I Spy Shapes in Art* by Lucy Mickelthwait, and *My Very First Book of Shapes* by Eric Carle

clear bins

lacing materials

puzzles

stacking materials

variety of geometric shapes

variety of materials for fine motor development

---

1. Open shelves look cluttered and distract the children from the manipulatives.

2. Inexpensive bamboo shades cover teacher-only storage.

Teacher's Comments

- Rearranging space to create a center for fine motor manipulatives has invited the children to play with the materials on display.
- Covering storage on shelves helps the children to focus on the materials available for their work.
- I am thrilled with the level of interest the children have in the new areas. They are engaging with the materials and staying engaged for longer periods of time. Before the change, there were days when no one wanted to play in any of these centers because the centers were not well defined and may have been visually overwhelmed by the bookshelf.

Child's Comment

- I like the connecting cubes. I can make happy things with them.

Water

Developing a Vision

Why do you want to redo this area of the classroom?
I learned from my classroom observations that students are drawn to this area, so I would like to capitalize on the learning experiences here.

What learning would you like to take place in this part of your classroom?
I would like to see small-group cooperation and negotiation as well as communication skills, problem-solving skills, and higher-order thinking.

What is working that you would like to keep?
The water table area is in place, but needs to be defined. The area contains some tools for experimentation and measurement.

What are your concerns?
I will be challenged to maintain the center and observe play. I would like to see tools added as students' needs and interests expand.

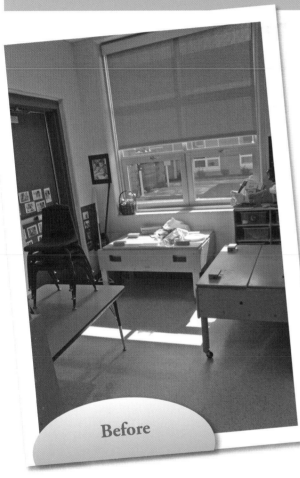

Before

Description of the Classroom

This clean, shiny, and uncluttered PreK classroom is being used for the first time this year. Things are clean, shiny, and uncluttered. Because of the newness of the area, the arrangement, displays, and material collections are still being developed. The sand-and-water area is well placed next to a row of large windows that have shades for diffusing the natural light during bright periods of the day. There is a wooden water table with a drain and top as well as a separate sand table that also has a cover. The manipulatives available include measuring cups, miniature animals, and other small tools and props. The basics for an effective area are present, but more props and tools are needed to encourage longer periods of engagement.

Plan of Action

- Survey the tools and props that are stored and/or displayed in the classroom. Determine which items extend play and which provide additional opportunities to learn the properties of water or sand.

- Soften the space and make it more interesting by adding translucent draping fabric, mobiles, or other items to provide visual interest.

- Find ways to display the tools so the children can determine what items they want to use and where to put them when they are finished.

- Obtain a waterproof cover for the floor that can go under the water table and contain the water.

- Gather materials to place on the tables besides water and sand, such as soil, snow, pebbles, foam peanuts, shredded paper, and colored water.

- Collect books that relate to sand or water, such as *Water* by Dorling Kindersley, *Water* by Frank Asch, *Sun Dance, Water Dance* by Jonathan London, *We Use Water* by Robin Nelson, and *The Sun, the Wind, and the Rain* by Lisa Westberg Peters.

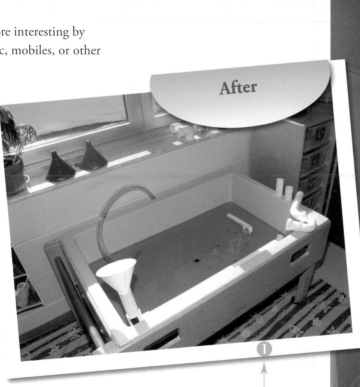

1. The brightly colored water encourages exploration and experimentation.

2. A clear shoe rack offers easy access to PVC pipes. Pictures of classmates using the water area inspire others to join the fun.

After

Store and display tools on pegboard with pictures, so the children can return the tools easily.

Center Drawing: Water

FABRIC OVERHANG

CABINET W/ TOYS

PIPES

PICTURES

KITCHEN UTENSILS

WATER TABLE

Materials to Add

2–3 yards of sheer fabric (depending on the size of the area)

clear plastic tubing of various sizes (so the children can see the colored water move through the tubes)

clear shoe racks to hold the tools (to display on the wall next to the table)

clear shower curtain liner (to place on the floor under the water or sand table)

digital pictures of children using the tools in the water area (to display on the wall near the table to inspire new ways of manipulating the water and sand)

measuring cups, spoons

variety of sizes of PVC pipe and fittings (including one that attaches to the side of the table so the children can pour water through the pipe into the water table)

variety of small containers

Special Feature

Made of a two-yard piece of fabric purchased at a local discount store, the drape adds softness and identifies the space as the water area. This fabric was sprayed (outside of the classroom while the children were not present) with a flame-retardant liquid, then dried. Next, each end of the fabric was stapled to a 1"-diameter dowel rod. In the center of the fabric, another dowel rod equal in length to the dowels on each end was used to support the fabric drape. All dowel rods were hung the appropriate distance from the fluorescent lights using fishing line. To add to the interest, blue child-safe bath pellets were added to the water in the table.

Teacher's Comments

- The children love the new space. They are excited about the measuring tools and the opportunity to experiment with a variety of materials.
- The sign-up sheet is a big hit.
- The children brainstorm ideas and work together to build with pipes and clear tubes.
- Children use rich conversation and new vocabulary as they engage in water play. An example of how they are learning is demonstrated by this observation: One child was looking at the tubes and asked the teacher how to put water in a small tube. The teacher suggested that he could figure out how to do it. First, he put the small tube into the big tube and saw that didn't work. Then he tried to use the funnel but the tube was smaller than the end of the funnel; it didn't work either. Finally, he got the baster and figured out that, by squeezing and releasing, he could fill the tube with water. It was the perfect size to fill the tube. He experimented, problem solved, and was successful at finding a solution to his problem in the Water Center.

Children's Comments

- It's so much fun to put the beads in the pipes and put water in, too. Then the beads shoot out. I think the beads, pipes, and everything are so cool.
- I like to make tunnels out of the pipes and watch the water fly out.

Math

Developing a Vision

Why do you want to redo this area of the classroom?
I want the children to be excited about mathematics and see it as a conquerable challenge. If I am working with them in the area, they seem comfortable and they participate, but they are hesitant to choose the Math Center on their own.

What learning would you like to take place in this part of your classroom?
Many things, including problem solving; small motor development; working independently and with others; and math concepts such as numbers, shapes, and patterns.

What is working that you would like to keep?
The children are interested in puzzles and things that fit together. They also enjoy working with peg boards for counting and number identification.

What are some ideas you have for improving the space?
I am open. It does need something special that will draw the children to the math/manipulatives area.

What are your concerns?
The children are not choosing to go to this area during center time. If they do go, the amount of time they stay is very limited.

Before

Description of the Classroom

This is a PreK classroom that is funded by the state. Because it is a new space, there is little clutter in the classroom. A wall of large windows provides natural light, and sun shades provide relief from the bright light at certain times of the day. Storage is available in large colored cabinets on one wall that also contains a child's sink. The room is arranged with a large-group meeting place and a number of centers that are functioning effectively. Tile covers the floors throughout the space. Appropriate materials are grouped in the areas where they will be used, making them easily accessible. However, because the materials are in baskets in the bookcase, it is difficult for the children to see the choices that are available to them. Some work is displayed on the walls, including pictures of the children. Because this is a new space, the wall displays are only beginning to appear.

Plan of Action

- Create an attractive and meaningful way to draw the children's interest to the math/manipulatives space. Place a featured material out on the table so the children can see what is available rather than having everything in baskets in the bookcase.

- Review the materials that are available in this area, and determine what additional manipulatives are needed.

- Make the area more visually interesting for the children by adding an area rug, hanging items, and plants.

- Use state curriculum guidelines in the area of math and small motor development to determine and encourage specific learning objectives for the area.

- Demonstrate the possibilities and inspire exploration by displaying pictures of the children working with manipulatives.

- Provide time to for the class to plan, do, and reflect. Talk about the potential play activities in the math/manipulatives area during group time as the children are planning and making choices. After center time, discuss what the children did in centers, including what happened in the math/manipulatives area.

After

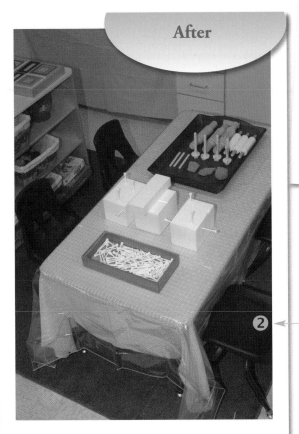
After

②

1. Attractive, clearly labeled baskets store some manipulatives.

2. Two activities are displayed on the table to invite children's participation.

③

3. Clear umbrellas with numbers and corresponding items add visual interest and clearly define the space.

After

Special Feature

To draw the children's interest, three clear umbrellas were suspended over the math/manipulatives area. One umbrella has a different number on each section and an equal number of items hanging underneath. Another umbrella displays shapes for the children to see from another perspective. The third umbrella has patterns repeated on the different sections. These umbrellas, with number elements, visually identify the area and inspire interest in the math concepts and materials.

The table display offers interesting activities and materials to use on a specific day. Other materials remain in the baskets on the shelf and are clearly labeled and easily accessible. Displaying some materials helps the children see new possibilities that are not visible when everything is stored away. The combinations of clay and tools and foam pieces and golf tees are particularly enticing to young children, when these items are attractively displayed in trays on a tablecloth in the area.

Materials to Add

additional manipulatives that are interesting for young children

area rug (to soften the area and identify the space that is used for math/manipulatives)

clear plastic umbrellas (hung from the ceiling to identify the location of the math area)

tablecloth (to add visual interest to displayed items)

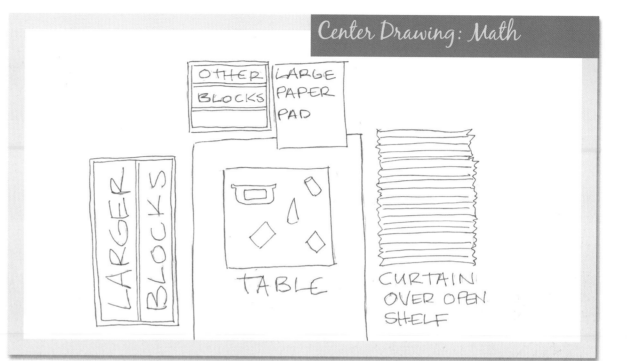

Center Drawing: Math

Teacher's Comments

- I think it is important for the Math Center to be defined and inviting. The umbrellas intrigued the children and they wanted to explore and investigate in the area. When there is a physical change in the environment children are eager to experiment with the new surroundings.
- The children definitely showed more interest in the Math Center following the changes.
- The apples were a big hit throughout the year. They counted them, classified them by size, and used them as symbols for money.
- The pegs in the Styrofoam were used for exploring math skills such as one-to-one correspondence. The children also used the pegs in creative ways, as the pegs became money and even robots.

Children's Comments

- The new umbrellas can be used if it rains; that's nice.
- Look, there are two scissors hanging on the number 2!
- Let's sell the apples. How many do we have? (said as the children count the number of apples)
- The children line the apples up and count out five. "Give me three dollars if you want to buy these." (Pegs are used as the money.)

Science

Developing a Vision

Why do you want to redo this area of the classroom?
It looks like the forgotten center. We want to increase the children's interest in science and in exploring natural materials.

What learning would you like to take place in this part of your classroom?
We would like to encourage curiosity, investigation, and longer interest in projects.

What is working that you would like to keep?
We have a good location for the Science Center in the corner of the room. We want to keep our fish and mice that we have in the area.

What are your concerns?
We have a number of two-and-a-half-year-olds in the classroom, so the materials, props, and activities need to be appropriate for their developmental level. We have discussed the possibility of a portable component to the center that could be taken outside. We would also like more natural materials and more habitats.

Before

Description of the Classroom

This is a large, open classroom with several windows that provide natural light. The teachers selected an appropriate space for the science area in the corner of the classroom. The walls are painted off-white, and the tile is brown. The area has fluorescent lights, which are turned off when natural light is available. There are two electrical outlets in the area. Some animals, including mice and fish, are in the existing area. Children in the classroom range from two-and-a-half to four years of age.

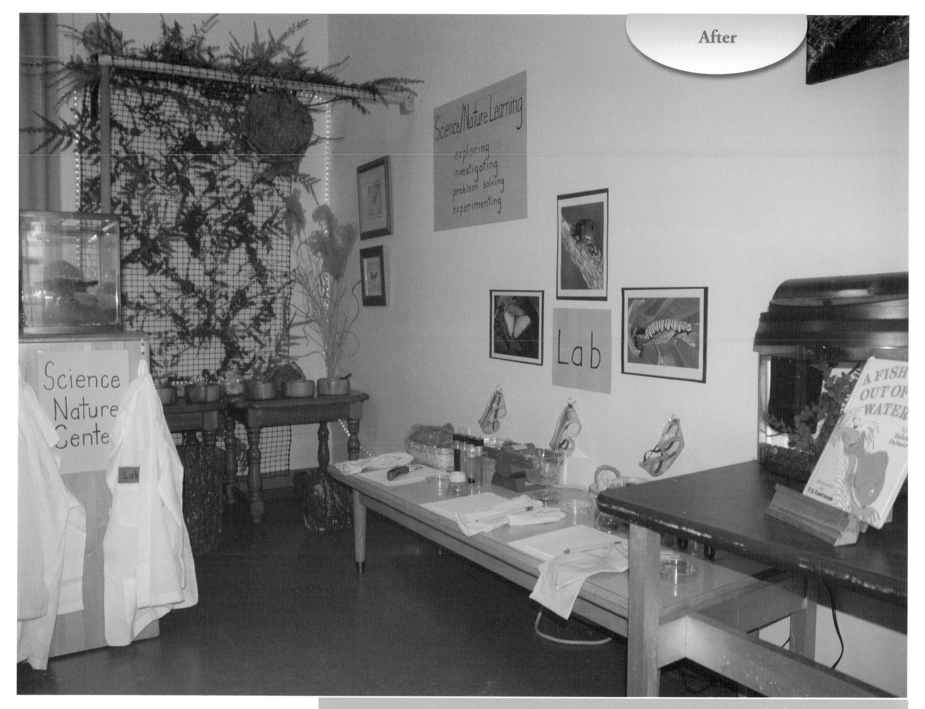

After

Science/Nature Learning

exploring
investigating
problem solving
experimenting

Lab

Science
Nature
Center

Lab

A FISH
OUT OF
WATER

Plan of Action

- Create a wall hanging using green landscaping fabric. Extend the wall hanging out over the area, creating a canopy over part of the center and add collections of natural materials to the canopy to create a special place to explore nature items.
- Group and rearrange materials found in the classroom or storage area that are related to science exploration
- Create a worm farm using an existing aquarium.
- Collect a variety of natural materials to include during each season. For example, in autumn, these could include acorns, pinecones, stones, and leaves.
- Find items related to insects to display in the area. These may include pictures, models, and live examples.
- Provide seating for the children to use when they examine items in the nature area.
- Explore ways to add lighting to the area because it is located in a dark corner of the classroom. Possibilities for improving lighting include adding a sturdy floor lamp, a clip-on light, or rope lighting.

1. Real tree-stump stools add unique seating in the discovery area.

2. Lab coats, goggles, and gloves support role-playing "scientists."

3. An old suitcase lined with plastic and filled with dirt creates a unique place to dig for plastic bugs.

Materials to Add

aquarium and potting soil (for insects and worms)

artificial greenery pieces (to wind through the holes of the green landscape cloth)

children's books and reference books about bugs, worms, and nature

3 clipboards and pencils (for writing notes from observations or experiments conducted in the area)

goggles (for experiments)

lab coats (for dressing up)

large roll of green landscape cloth

large wooden stumps (used for sitting, to coordinate with the nature theme. Make stumps safe by painting with nonflammable polyurethane, in a safe area when the children are not around)

rope lighting (to add interest and light up the area)

unbreakable beakers (for pouring)

Teacher's Comments

- I am so pleased with our new "lab" (Science Center). Observing the children in their investigation of bugs and natural materials has led to further expansion of the center. We added more books, puppets, and real bugs.

- Our excitement about the new center has resulted in the children's parents asking us how they might help. One family donated a snake skin and another dug up worms for our worm habitat.

- The children determine whether they can go into the lab by checking the number of lab coats hanging on hooks or being worn by their classmates. They are able to manage independently the number of people who can be in the area.

- I knew our Science Center needed more attention, and our new "lab" has answered many of my concerns. We added books, writing tablets, and clipboards to boost literacy and writing opportunities. Caring for our new corn plant has given the children a sense of responsibility and ownership as well.

- The center has remained intact because the children are careful to put items back in their original spaces. We added more baskets to hold the yellow gloves and pencils. These help the children with cleanup.

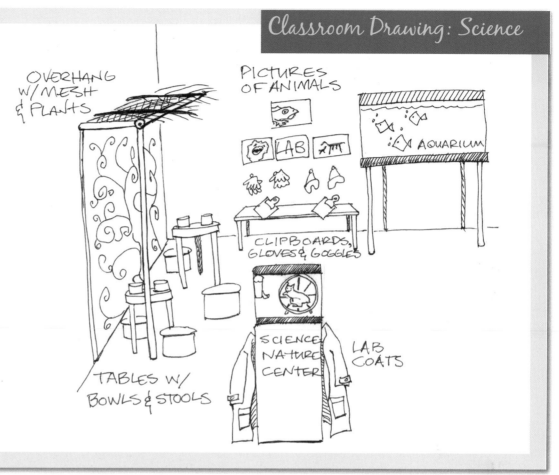

Classroom Drawing: Science

OVERHANG W/ MESH & PLANTS

PICTURES OF ANIMALS

LAB

AQUARIUM

CLIPBOARDS, GLOVES & GOGGLES

SCIENCE NATURE CENTER

LAB COATS

TABLES W/ BOWLS & STOOLS

Child's Comment

- My dad is a scientist. (Father is a surgeon and wears a lab coat.) This is my favorite center.

Music and Performance

Developing a Vision

Why do you want to redo this area of the classroom?

This is the "leftover" area. We have a collection of lots of things but not really the instruments we need. Our children like to perform and do productions, so we thought we could build on their interests.

What learning would you like to take place in this part of your classroom?

We would like to enhance the children's creativity, while developing their love for music. This would be a good place to complete a sequence of steps: plan a show, select costumes and instruments, present the music, and clean up the area.

What is working that you would like to keep?

We have a large space and some instruments.

What are your concerns?

The area needs to be more defined. A recording studio with headphones for listening or recording would be great, and so would unbreakable mirrors so the children could see themselves on stage.

Before

Description of Classroom

The classroom is in a large open space with several learning centers that function effectively. Large arched windows are an excellent source of natural light. The walls that separate the space from other classrooms do not go to the ceiling, which means that sound is an issue. The classroom has little storage, but there is a large storage area for materials and supplies across the hall from the space. Mobiles hanging in the area provide additional interest. The classroom includes both carpet and tile for quiet or messy activities. The children in the space are three-year-olds, with a few newly turned four-year-olds.

On the whiteboard: Performance by:

On the pegboard: INSTRUMENTS

Plan of Action

- Collect all existing musical instruments and determine what additional items are needed to provide a variety of sounds and rhythms. Include melody, rhythm, and percussion instruments and a keyboard. Determine how these will be displayed so the children can see the selection of instruments and choose the ones they want to use.
- Build a stage to identify the music space. The raised area helps the children recognize where the practices and performances occur. Using varied heights helps distribute the sound produced on the stage and can lower the sound level in the open spaces.

  Note: It is easy to construct a stage with two pallets. The pallets provide the foundation for the stage. Cover the pallets with a half sheet of ¼" plywood. Cover the plywood with carpet, or paint it brown or gray. This area, raised 3–4" off the floor, provides a special place for music and drama productions.
- Obtain costumes, fabric, and dancing shoes to inspire the performing music groups and to encourage audience participation.
- Obtain a large refrigerator box to transform into a recording studio. Locate or purchase a player/recorder to use inside the box with other appropriate items.
- Create props, such as curtains that can be hung behind the stage, microphones, and other appropriate items, that will help children recognize the area as a music and performance place.

1. A cardboard box becomes a special place for children to record their music.

2. An African mobile moves and adds visual interest to the area.

1. A mirror and instruments encourage movement and participation.

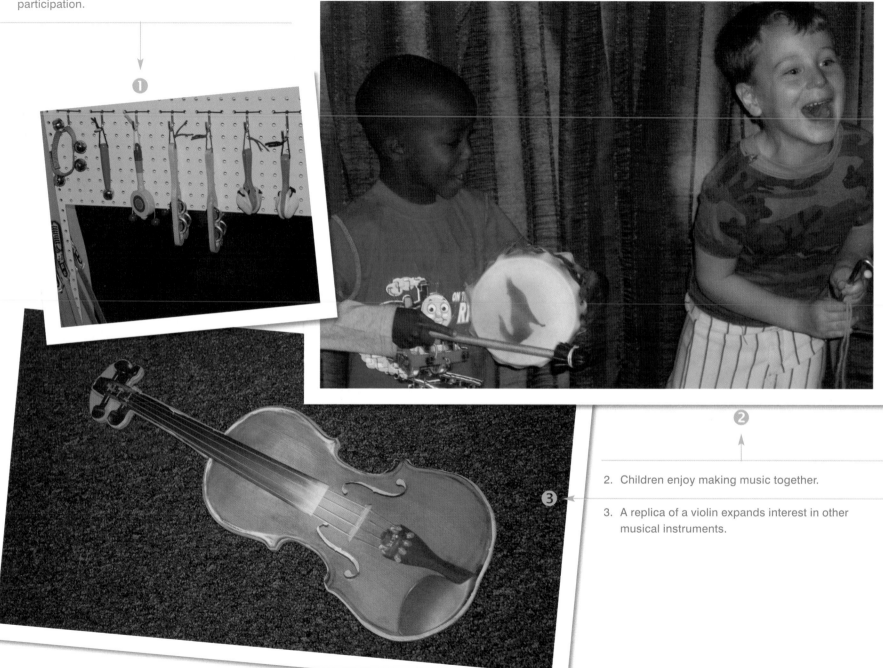

2. Children enjoy making music together.

3. A replica of a violin expands interest in other musical instruments.

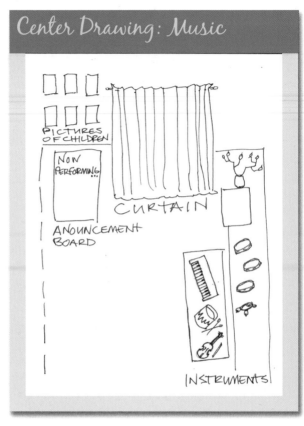

Center Drawing: Music

PICTURES OF CHILDREN

NOW PERFORMING...

ANOUNCEMENT BOARD

CURTAIN

INSTRUMENTS

Materials to Add

collection of musical instruments, including drums, maracas, stick bells, rhythm sticks, guiro, xylophone, keyboard, and guitar

literacy items, including sheet music, books of songs, staff paper for writing music, paper and markers (to create programs, posters of shows, and to write names of performers)

music and instruments that relate to the cultures of the children in the classroom

performance microphones, purchased or made

tape player/recorder with microphone and tapes (to record child-created songs)

variety of costumes, including pieces of fabric, unusual hats, tap shoes, and ballet slippers

Teacher's Comment

● We've had many creative performances in the new center. One of the children has great difficulty speaking and communicating with others, which makes him hesitant to talk and express his ideas in a group setting. In the Music Center, he put on a cowboy hat, grabbed the microphone, and went on the stage where he confidently sang "Old MacDonald Had a Farm" with every word clearly pronounced. For that moment, he became the performer in the Music Center, singing on the stage.

Children's Comments

● When the children were asked what they like about the Music Center, they responded: "I like everything," "the sparkly blue hats," "the stage," "the fancy costumes and dresses," "the best was the microphone," and "the recording studio."

Art Studio

Before

Developing a Vision

Why do you want to redo this area of the classroom?
I want to work on this area of my classroom because the children seem very interested in art. Although I have made some additions to the area, it is still not working.

What learning would you like to take place in this part of your classroom?
I would like to focus on creative thinking, fine motor skills, and expressing ideas.

What is working that you would like to keep?
The area is spacious and has two walls of closed cabinet space for storage. There is a child-level sink and surrounding counter space. The area is supplied with a variety of paints, brushes, and paper.

What are your concerns?
I would like the materials to be more accessible to the children, so they can use them independently. The art materials also need to be more organized, so the children can clean up and return things to their places when they finish using them.

Description of Classroom

This is a large classroom with a wall of windows that produces good natural light for the space. The back wall, which is within the Art Studio, is covered with cabinets that all have doors. There is a sink in the bottom unit of cabinets on this wall. The room is a neutral color, but the cabinets are a bright coral color that cannot be changed. The Art Studio has tiled floors and two tables with children's chairs, fluorescent lighting, and one electrical outlet.

After

Our Gallery

Featured Artist

Our Gallery

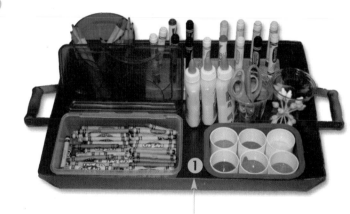

Plan of Action

- Declutter the area, determining which items to keep and which to store or discard.
- Develop a plan for making effective use of the space, creating engaging activities, and making the Art Studio environment more inspiring.
- Collect clear containers, a variety of tools, many types and sizes of paper, a scrap container, and copies of master artists' work.
- Plan ways for children to clean up easily.
- Decide on a featured artist and which of his or her works to display. Select appropriate techniques and materials that relate to his or her work.
- Hang a large canvas for the children, so they can create a mural over an extended period of time. The canvas will add to the authenticity of the children's work as they use real materials in their creations.
- Put trays containing glue, scissors, and markers on the table for easy access by children.
- Purchase a drying rack or bookcase that can hold work in progress. This will encourage the children to return to their work and will build more sustained interest.
- Create a gallery of the children's art, framed and beautifully displayed, on the two large cabinets in the art area. This will clearly demonstrate that their work is wonderful and valued in this space.
- Provide clay and tools on a table in the Art Studio. This will add the opportunity to explore a new art medium and will encourage the creation of three-dimensional projects.
- Add plants to soften the area.
- Include clear containers with attractive items to provide visual stimuli for the classroom artists.

1. A metal tray holds art materials for easy accessibility.

2. The children's art, beautifully displayed in the gallery.

3. A clear shoe rack offers a variety of painting tools.

Materials to Add

block of potter's clay and tools such as rolling pins, dowel rods, and cookie cutters to use with clay

bookcase (for storage or works in progress)

canvas material, 2 yards or more, stretched on a frame

featured artist's books and artwork (For example, *Hans Hofmann* by Cynthia Goodman or *Color Creates Light: Studies with Hans Hofmann* by Tina Dickey)

felt-covered wooden blocks (to use on the canvas and on paper to create designs inspired by the artist's work)

large, substantial, metal trays (to provide a portable display of art materials for the children to use independently)

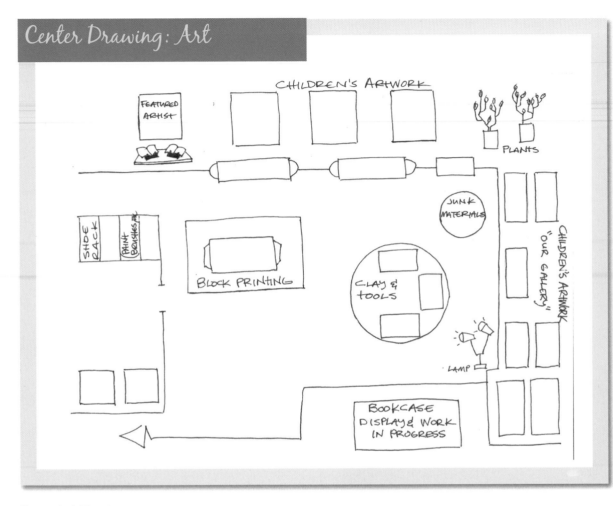

Special Feature

The first featured artist in the studio is Hans Hofmann. The children can view a collection of his work in books on display in the Art Studio, and can explore his techniques and materials as they use block shapes of color on a large canvas. After several days of adding prints to the picture, it is displayed on the wall for the group to admire. The featured artist in this area will change over the year to expand the children's exposure to different artists and to encourage opportunities to view, enjoy, and emulate a variety of art.

Teacher's Comments

- I have witnessed more creativity and independence with our new Art Studio. My children have come up with many ideas: "I would like to make a stained-glass house," or "I want to make a tree that sticks up off the paper."
- We now have our supplies organized so I can easily help the children find what they need, or the children can find it on their own.
- The children are more adventurous in their creations. As a teacher, it is so wonderful to watch the students engaged and immersed in a project.
- We are all learning more about art as we explore together and study our featured artist. We will continue to expose both the students and teachers to the significance and influence of art in our lives.

Children's Comments

- It's perfect!
- I love getting to paint with the new paintbrushes!
- It's like we have a whole new classroom!
- When are we going to get to work on our Hans Hofmann again?

Developing a Vision

Why do you want to redo this area of the classroom?

It is hard to keep Home Living interesting. We need some fresh ideas, a new arrangement of props, refurbishing of materials, perhaps prop boxes. We want to increase the children's engagement in the center.

What learning would you like to take place in this part of your classroom?

We would like to increase socio-dramatic play, social interactions, and literacy opportunities.

What is working that you would like to keep?

The center currently contains some furniture, appliances, and clothing, including hats and shoes.

What are your concerns?

The center needs more dress-up items for boys. The area should be more clearly defined and inviting. We do not have cooking utensils. The furniture needs to be repaired and updated, and food from many cultures should be added. If the space were larger, a greater variety of play could occur; for instance, the bed area with dolls might include a rocking chair and books for reading to baby.

Before

Description of Classroom

This preschool classroom for three- and four-year-olds is an open area with few walls or dividers. The walls are cream colored, and the carpet is blue-gray. There is a partial wall that defines the space but does not go to the ceiling. Several walls contain large windows with a view of outside the classroom. The noise level can be high when all the children are in the space and playing. There are a number of learning centers and collections of appropriate materials in the space. There is no water in the area, but an adjoining bathroom does provide water when needed. There are very few outlets.

After

A wooden, framed home defines the space. The sign can be changed according to the dramatic play taking place within.

Home Living

couch

Plan of Action

- Build a raised area to create a special space for Home Living. This structure can also be used for other dramatic play, as the center is transformed to a fire station or restaurant.
- Repair and reupholster the existing couch and chair.
- Collect clothing for the winter season, including items for males. Items could include hats, gloves, boots, heavy coats, and scarves.
- Locate or purchase additional dishes, pots, and pans.
- Warm up the area by adding pillows, throws, plants, and soft lighting.
- Add beautiful features that support the home environment, such as framed pictures of the children with their families, tablecloths, floral arrangements, and fabric hangings.
- Provide literacy materials, such as books to read to the baby, books and magazines for parents, and cookbooks in the cooking area. Include notepads and pens or markers for leaving messages.

1. Clear containers display beautiful natural materials. A metal vase was placed in front of a mirror to create interest.

2. The couch was reupholstered and softened with a pillow. Literacy items include magazines and an *Our Families* book.

1. Framed photos of the children and their parents personalize the space.

2. Boys are involved in socio-dramatic play as they cook dinner.

Center Drawing: Home Living

HOME LIVING

Teacher's Comments

- The children have enjoyed the new space so very, very much. The first question in the morning is, "Is Home Living open?"
- The children took the new clear containers and divided the fruits and vegetables. They were organizing and using math skills. They also had to problem-solve to fit everything into the containers.
- All of the children have really enjoyed the new space. The center has already been turned into a train station, a bus station, and a "hair cutting place."
- Of course, the babies continue to be a center theme.
- The boys and girls alike remain so excited about the center; it is the first place they choose to play.

Children's Comments

- I can make an apple pie!
- I like the new seats.

Special Feature

The framed house provides a large and visually identifiable space for the Home Living Center. It was built over a weekend with reused wood. The construction and painting crew included a grandfather, a teacher, students, and an author. The total cost of the structure was about one hundred dollars, which includes plywood for the flooring. This raised and visually interesting structure stimulates new play and learning opportunities in the classroom.

Materials to Add

collection of clothing (some donated by parents, some purchased in secondhand stores and garage sales)
collection of clothing items and housekeeping materials (currently in the classroom but not grouped together)
kitchen items (purchased): pots, pans, plates, and eating utensils
recycled books, magazines, notepads, and other writing materials
sturdy floor lamp (by the couch for reading)
wood and plywood for the frame of the house
wooden frames (for pictures of the children and families)

Developing a Vision

Before

Why do you want to change this area of the classroom?

We have been using the Home Living Center for a while. Because we don't have much space, we would like to change this area into a different center. The children and teachers are interested in setting up a Fire Station. Some of the furniture and props in the Home Living area work in a fire station, so the transition should be relatively easy. This new center, in the Home Living space, will provide an environment that will nurture learning experiences related to firefighters and community helpers.

What learning would you like to take place in this part of your classroom?

I hope the Fire Station will be engaging for our children. Following their interests, they should learn about their community, including what firefighters do, and practice solving problems together. I also have some books about firefighters that can provide a literacy element.

What is working that you would like to keep?

The Home Living area works well because the structure and materials encourage play about homes and families. When we change [to a new focus], some furniture, props, and materials that were in Home Living area can be used in the Fire Station center.

What are your ideas for improvement?

To organize the new materials in the familiar space so the children can make real-life connections though play.

Plan of Action

- Select props and furniture from the Home Living area that will remain in the center when it becomes the Fire Station Center.
- Collect or purchase dress-up items for firefighters: helmets, gloves, boots, and yellow rain jackets.
- Find maps of the local area to be displayed in the Fire Station Center.
- Provide old cell phones, walkie-talkies, phone books, and clipboards for taking calls.
- Add books about firefighters to the center, such as *Fire Truck* by Peter Sis, *Big Frank's Fire Truck* by Leslie McGuire, *I Want to Be a Firefighter* by Dan Liebman, and *The Little Fire Engine* by Lois Lenski.
- Display pictures of firefighters.
- Provide a short piece of hose with a nozzle.
- Use baskets to display some props.
- Make a message board, and include markers and sticky notepads (for leaving messages for the next shift of firefighters).

1. The frame structure and space used for the Home Living Center is transformed into a Fire Station Center.

2. Boots, gloves, and a hose are ready for the firefighters.

3. The desk and the map are more real elements in the Fire Station Center. They provide a place for writing and for locating familiar places on the community map.

Materials to Add

3–4 books about firefighters

cell phone and/or walkie-talkie

2–3 firefighter helmets

garden hose, small section with a nozzle

maps and writing pads

2–3 pairs of rubber boots

whiteboard and washable marker (for leaving
    messages)

Teacher's Comments

● Since we built the new structure for the Home
    Living area, we have been talking about what
    other centers could work in this area. One idea,
    suggested by several teachers, was the Fire Station
    Center. I am so glad we changed the Home Living
    Center into the Fire Station Center, because it
    stimulates such a different kind of play. Now we
    have training for firefighters; they are taking calls,
    putting out fires, and relaxing in the center.

● The children are collaborating and using new
    vocabulary that relates to this theme. We are not
    sure how long the Fire Station Center will be up
    before we go back to the Home Living Center, but
    we will observe the children's interest to help us
    decide.

Children's Comments

● I will take the call and tell you where to go for the
    fire.

● Put on the boots and coat. Now we can put out
    the fire.

● This book has a picture of a fire truck. A dog is
    riding on it. Did you see the hose? We have a fire
    station close to my house.

Restaurant

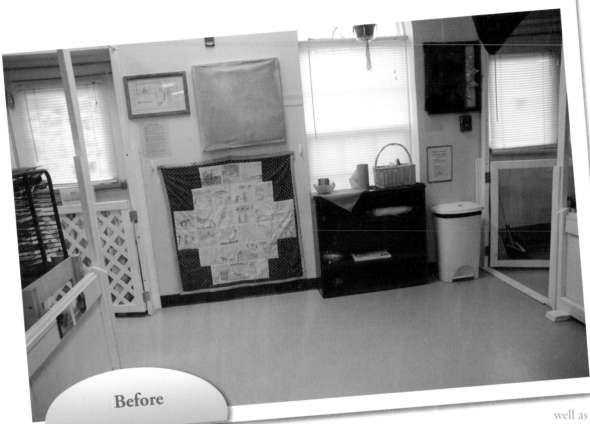

Before

Developing a Vision

Why do you want to change this area of the classroom?
The Restaurant will facilitate social interactions among three to four children. Children can use printed materials and can create their own writing as they take orders and collect money.

What learning would you like to take place in this part of your classroom?
I would like the center to provide opportunities for role-playing specific tasks related to a restaurant. The social protocols of eating in a restaurant can be modeled and experienced. Children can learn about foods that reflect many cultures.

What is working that you would like to keep?
The space is inviting, with an outside window and barriers that define the area on two sides. The center has tables and chairs that can be moved to the area, as well as child-sized kitchen equipment and a cash register.

What are your concerns?
The area where the Restaurant will be located is open with low dividers separating it from the rest of the classroom. This could make noise an issue in the Restaurant.

What are your ideas for improvement?
I hope this area will provide exposure to environmental print and literacy with the use of signs and menus.

Description of Classroom

This preschool classroom is located in the preschool wing of a child care center that serves infants through five-year-olds. The classroom space is open, with learning centers that are identified and separated by low boundaries, including lattice work and low dividers. Plants hang in the light coming through large, arched windows. The walls are off-white, and part of the area has tile for messy activities. Another portion of the classroom has commercial carpet that is blue and brown and is used for group time, library, and other activities.

The kitchen provides many literacy opportunities including menus, posters of prices, pizza boxes, and books about pizza making. Chef hats encourage role playing.

After

Open

Recipe
3½ cups flour
1½ cups hot water
½ cup vegetable oil

Makes 12 servings

Louigi's
Pizza

Louigi's
Cheese
Pepperoni
Mushroom
Veggie

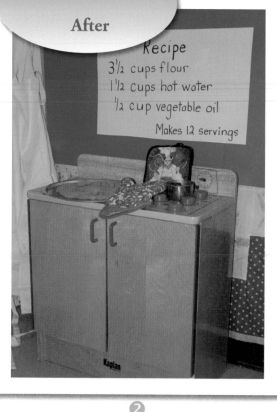

Plan of Action

- Collect props for the Restaurant from the classroom, other preschool areas, and the storage area.
- Determine what type of restaurant the children would like to add to their classroom. (A pizza place was selected.)
- Purchase tablecloths and other decorations for the area.
- Bring plants into the area to create a homey atmosphere.
- Collect menus, pizza boxes, and other printed materials that relate to the Restaurant and connect to the children's experience.
- Make signs showing the items available and their cost, including pictures, words, and prices.
- Find or make play money for the cash register.
- Collect dress-up items or make props such as chef hats and aprons.

1. The check-out area includes a sign, cash register, and money for paying.

2. The cooking area displays a simple recipe and includes pizza pans and aprons for the chefs.

Materials to Add

cash register with play money

pads and pencils (for taking orders)

pizza pans, rolling pins, cutters, measuring cups, and pizza boxes

plants and flowers (to make the space attractive)

poster board and pictures (to make menus and signs, such as open/closed, and advertisements)

potter's clay (for making pizzas)

tablecloths

white fabric and poster board (to make chef hats)

Center Drawing: Restaurant

Teacher's Comments

- It is so interesting to observe the children in their play around the Pizza Place theme. Many roles are used, including chef, waiter, money taker, customer, and taster.

- Opportunities to develop literacy are everywhere—writing orders, reading menus, and making the recipe for pizza.

- The children are very interested and engaged in the Pizza Place operations and cooperate to make things work. The interest is so high, I may keep the area set up for longer than the two weeks originally planned.

Children's Comments

- I like making the pizza out of clay.

- This is just like the pizza place near my house; we order take-outs, too.

- Some of the waiters need training.

- When we have pizza for lunch, we can eat it in our place.

- When can we have a Chinese Restaurant?

Before

Developing a Vision

Why do you want to change this area of your classroom?

I want to have a place where the children can be more focused during community time. In this space we meet in the morning, talk about the day, read a story, check the calendar, and return for other meeting times.

What learning would you like to take place in this part of your classroom?

I would like the children to concentrate on a story, to listen to others, and be attentive for a longer period of time.

What is working that you would like to keep?

We need to keep the calendar because that is one of the skills identified in our kindergarten guidelines. I love my rocker that I got many years ago when I lived in England. I like having all my teacher resources in the two bookcases at the front of the room. My teacher materials are organized by theme and stored in large plastic containers in the bookcases.

What are your concerns?

During circle time, children are not focusing on the story or the activities. They are distracted and pulling on each other. Throughout the time we are meeting, the children are wiggling and crawling around. I would like them to be more focused on what is happening during the community time and while making plans for the day.

Description of the Classroom

This is a kindergarten class located in an elementary school. In this large classroom, there are 21 kindergarten children, a teacher, and an aide. The teacher has collected many wonderful materials and items in this classroom over many years. Currently, the space at the front of the room is used for large-group meetings throughout the day. The teacher would like the meeting place to remain in this location.

Plan of Action

- Determine the placement of the community Gathering Place.
- Clear the area of all materials, and then determine what stays and what goes.
- Cover the bookcases in the area with curtains on tension rods. Use the bookcases to store materials that the children are not using. For example, covering containers of books related to specific units of study removes this visual distraction from the Gathering Place.
- Take pictures of the children with a digital camera and display the photos in the Gathering Place. As seen in so many classrooms in Reggio, photographs of the children show who lives in this space
- Prepare a display of the teacher's picture, and photos of family, pets, and things of interest. This framed display recognizes the teacher as an important member of the community, with unique talents.
- The entire wall of the Gathering Place is covered with whiteboard, and only a portion of it is used on a regular basis. Plan to cover half of the whiteboard with a calm, neutral fabric to soften the area and provide an additional display area.
- Keep the teacher's special items, such as the wooden chair and nesting tables. These treasures make the space unique for this teacher.
- Place a small lamp, providing soft light, on the nesting tables to make the space more inviting.

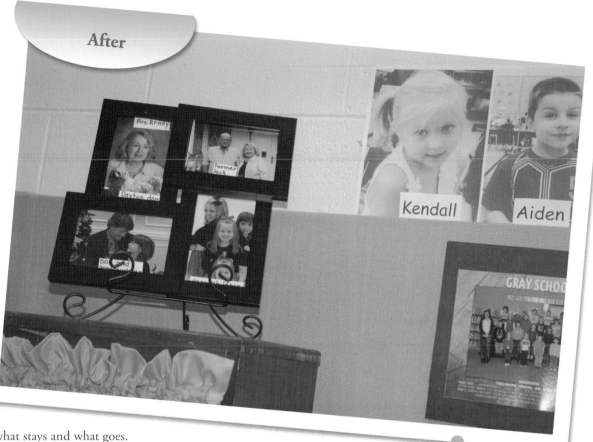

Photographs of the teacher, of her family and pets, and of the children communicate information about who lives in this classroom.

Kendall   Aiden   Riley   Bethany   Haley   Tanner   Alexis   Chase   Storm

After

Our Community

A large collage frame holds many pictures of the children participating in activities.

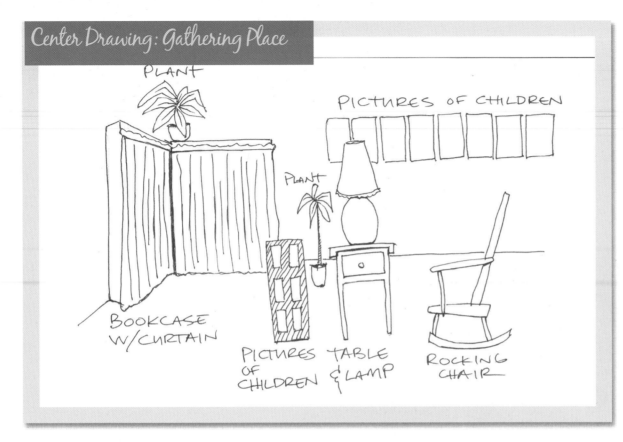

Center Drawing: Gathering Place

PLANT

PICTURES OF CHILDREN

PLANT

BOOKCASE W/CURTAIN

PICTURES OF CHILDREN

TABLE & LAMP

ROCKING CHAIR

Materials to Add

additional lighting

different rug for the floor

fabric to cover the whiteboard

frames for photos of the teacher and the children

pictures of the children

plants

sheer curtains to cover teacher resources in the bookcase

Teacher's Comments

- I am very pleased with the results. It has changed the classroom climate. The children are much more attentive.
- Behavior has been much better during community (group) time. Because of this project, I took down my behavior chart. I am not going to put it back; I haven't needed it.
- The whole room seems so much more spacious and inviting.

Other Teachers' and Parents' Comments

- It's fabulous.
- It makes the room seem so much bigger.
- Very nice, very homey.
- Several teachers who visited were thinking out loud about what they could do in their classroom.

Children's Comments

- Wow (as he touches all the new things). It's beautiful!
- I think my picture is very nice.
- I like it. I like it all!

Welcome Area

Before

Developing a Vision

Why do you want to change this area of your classroom?
The entrance to the classroom is uninviting, not very welcoming. It is important for the children to feel comfortable in the room. As they enter, children should feel the room belongs to them. The room should be more about the children, who they are, and their work.

What learning would you like to take place in this part of your classroom?
The entrance area can set the tone for the day. It can assist with establishing routines. Children learn responsibility as they deliver papers to appropriate bins upon entrance, sign in for attendance, and check job assignments.

What is working that you would like to keep?
Greeting the children as they enter the room works so well for setting a positive tone. It is especially helpful for greeting bilingual children who are just beginning to acquire English language skills. A smile from the teacher in the Welcome Area sends the message that the child's presence is important.

What are your concerns?
It is important to keep an open pathway for the entrance area.

Description of the Classroom

This kindergarten classroom is located in an elementary school building that was built in 1981. It has one window beside the exterior door, but there is not a lot of natural light because the covered walkway outside blocks the light. The entrance to the room is a large opening with no door. The building is circular, and the classrooms are not completely closed. A moveable wall closes this classroom off from the next. Along one wall, near the entrance, there are fixed cabinets. The classroom has no sinks or bathrooms and has a floor covered with a mixture of rug and tile space. The entrance area to the classroom is neither inviting nor representative of the 20 kindergarten children and one teacher who live and work within the room.

Plan of Action

- Remove the big furniture.
- Get rid of excess furniture.
- Remove the storage items.
- Add photos of the children learning.
- Add plants.
- Add clipboards for sign in.
- Personalize the space for the children.
- Add a "welcome" sign.

Before

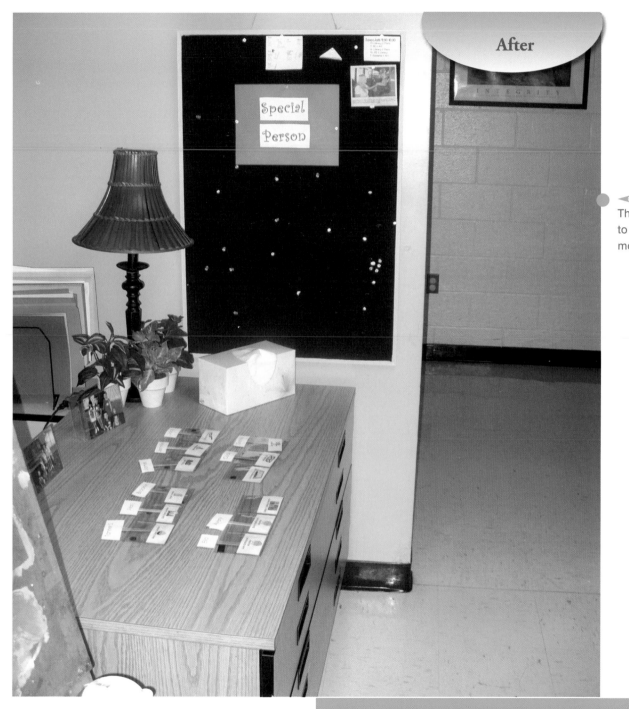

The bulletin board in this area provides plenty of space to highlight individual children and help the class learn more about one another.

1. With the larger, heavy furniture removed, the entrance area is open and designed for the children's use.

2. Casual snapshots capture the children learning and living within the classroom.

3. Clipboards make sign-in easy.

②

③

Center: Welcome Area

PICTURES OF CHILDREN

PLANT

WELCOME

DOOR

TABLE W/ CLIPBOARDS

Teacher's Comment

- By seeing photos of themselves engaged in learning experiences, the children feel a sense of belonging as they enter the room. In addition, other stakeholders, including parents, administrators, and other teachers, see the learning taking place.

Child's Comment

- Oh, look—I was measuring apples in that picture.

Special Feature

The special feature for this area is the representation of those who live and work in the space. The children enjoy seeing themselves in the photographs on the wall as they enter, and they reflect upon their experiences. Families see the work that occurs during the learning day as they arrive and pick up the children. Other visitors immediately know what is happening in this classroom as they come in.

Materials to Add

bins (for parents to drop off signed forms)
clipboards and pencils (for sign-in)
hand sanitizer
job responsibility chart or choice board
photos of learners in action
plants (to add a welcoming touch)
tissues
welcome sign

Calming Place

Before

Developing a Vision

Why do you want to add this area to your classroom?
I need a space for the children to have some alone time, whether it's to adjust to starting the day or to calm themselves after being sad or upset.

What learning would you like to take place in this part of your classroom?
There are many possibilities for learning including self-regulation, emotional identification, problem solving, and finding a way to deal with conflict.

What is working that you would like to keep?
We use the picture schedule and solution kits (stories, emotion cards, and problem-solving situations) in the classroom. Currently, I do not have a quiet/private space for self-regulation and/or alone time.

What are your concerns?
We have a curriculum/program that works on emotional development, and I would like to incorporate some of the ideas from that curriculum. I want to create a space that is inviting and soothing, using soft lighting, soft music, and calming materials such as flowing fabric.

Description of the Classroom

This classroom is located in a new middle school facility. Three PreK classrooms are in a separate wing of the building, separated from the middle school students by a large gymnasium. This PreK classroom is a midsize space with large windows covering one wall. Fixed features include a wall of storage cabinets with top and bottom units and a counter, which provides work space. The counter contains a sink at the child's level. A shared bathroom divides the classrooms. Most of the furniture in the classroom is wooden and well designed, including a low table that can be used for working when standing as well as sitting. Because it is a new space, there are few items on the walls or hanging from the ceiling.

Using this chart, a child can identify his or her feelings and change the picture when he or she is calm.

Plan of Action

- Identify a space in the classroom that can be quiet and away from the active areas of the classroom. (For example, select some unused space next to the teacher's desk on a quiet side of the classroom.)
- Investigate possible structures that can be built inexpensively and that will provide a semi-enclosed space where a child can go when upset or tired.
- Order earphones that can be used with the existing tape/CD player.
- Collect items to soften the space, and provide soothing materials to help a child calm down when inside the structure. The child can select an item to hold and stroke when inside the dome. This allows the child to calm down and at his or her own pace.
- Create a mobile to hang in front of the large open windows in the identified space. This will add visual interest to the area.
- Make a feelings wheel to help the child identify the emotions that prompted him or her to come to this area. Include both words and pictures on the wheel, and make them easily identifiable. Use "calm" as one of the choices on the feelings wheel, allowing the child to choose that option as he or she leaves the center. This wheel provides a way for the child to name his or her feelings and determine when he or she is calm enough to rejoin the class.
- Place children's books that deal with emotions inside the structure. A few suggestions include *It's Okay to Be Different* by Todd Parr, *The Feelings Book* by Todd Parr, *When Sophie Gets Angry—Really, Really, Angry* by Molly Bang, *On Monday When It Rained* by Cheryl Kachenmeister, and *Alexander and the Terrible, Horrible, No Good, Very Bad Day* by Judith Viorst.

1. Pillows, soft toys, and blankets are soothing and comforting.

2. A hand-woven blanket from South America provides pattern and visual interest.

Special Feature

The dome structure provides a small cozy space where one child may go. This is a simple, inexpensive project constructed from wood and plywood, which volunteers built in a short period of time. In this classroom, a grandfather built the dome, and the teacher selected the fabric. The structure is covered with translucent fabric stapled to the top and draped over the sides to provide privacy but also visibility for the teacher to observe this space.

Materials to Add

baskets (to display and contain CDs, stuffed animals, and books)

CDs of soft relaxing music

CD player (simple enough so the children are able to operate it and use it with earphones)

children's books about feelings and emotions

colored pieces of plastic, fishing line, and loop (to create a mobile to hang in front of the large windows)

four lengths of 2" x 4" lumber and a sheet of plywood (for the dome structure)

mat or large cushion (to place on the floor of the dome to create a soft and inviting space)

pillows covered with soft touchable fabric

stuffed animals (to place in a basket inside the dome)

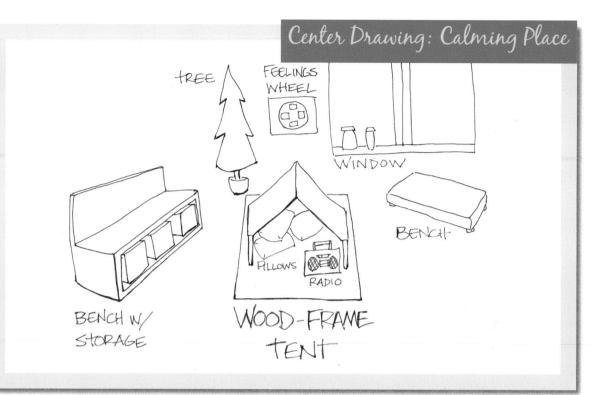

Center Drawing: Calming Place

Teacher's Comments

- The area is exactly what I wanted. I love the cozy feel of the fabric and the softness of the added materials and decoration.
- It is a lovely space that is very functional for our needs. The children are using the area effectively after our discussion about what was expected to happen there.
- I can offer a quiet space to the children. I remind them that this area is available and usable. My hope is that the children will remind each other about the space and independently will go to the area to solve conflicts or calm their feelings when difficulties arise.

Children's Responses

- The children were very excited about the quiet area. They were especially interested in the fabric that was draped over the top because they could see inside the dome.
- The children enjoyed covering up with the soft throw inside the dome and snuggling with a book.
- We read scripted stories about emotions, and we plan to add other stories that we create together.

Early Learning Standards
AND THE CLASSROOM ENVIRONMENT

One traditional way of planning in an early childhood classroom is for you to determine the learning objectives that you want to accomplish with the children during the year. The specific objectives for your group of children may be determined by the school system, a planned curriculum, a team of teachers, or an individual teacher. They may be stated in general terms, such as, "the children will expand their vocabulary," or in more measureable terms, such as, "the children will gain 25 new vocabulary words this year." As an effective teacher, you will use your knowledge of each child's developmental strengths and interests to adjust individual learning objectives and modify materials and activities for every child to be successful.

Early Learning Standards

K–12 and PreK classrooms are guided by curriculum standards. Forty-four states have adopted PreK standards to guide teachers as they design learning experiences. This fairly new process is mandatory in some states and voluntary in others (see preknow.org/educators/resource/meetingstandards.cfm). When states are designing, revising, and improving their standards, organizations such as the National Association for the Education of Young Children (NAEYC) provide guidance. *Early Learning Standards: Creating the Conditions for Success,* a position statement developed by the NAEYC in collaboration with The

National Association of Early Childhood Specialists in State Departments of Education (NAECS-SDE), states that learning standards can lead to quality learning experiences that will build a foundation for future academic and social competence. According this position statement, early learning standards must contain four essential features:

1. Effective early learning standards emphasize significant, developmentally appropriate content and outcomes.
2. Effective early learning standards are developed and reviewed through informed, inclusive processes.
3. Early learning standards gain their effectiveness through implementation and assessment practices that support all children's development in ethical, appropriate ways.
4. Effective early learning standards require a foundation of support for early childhood programs, professionals, and families.

It is now common practice for teachers to communicate to parents, administrators, and others how lessons and experiences in the classroom help children meet identified standards. Sharing this information helps these interested groups understand how intentional play experiences are learning experiences that support specific early learning standards and curriculum goals.

One kindergarten teacher interviews each child individually at the beginning of the year to inquire about what he or she wants to learn in kindergarten. The teacher creates a chart documenting the children's personal learning objectives, and interweaves the learning objectives of the children with the state-mandated early learning standards, making sure that each child's learning objective is explored at some point throughout the year. This is one example of meeting mandated standards in a meaningful way for young learners. The last chapter of this book (see pages 127–148) describes a full-classroom makeover that includes how standards can be met as children play/work in a newly transformed kindergarten environment.

The Unique Needs of Children

Young children develop rapidly. Genetics and the environment (nature and nurture) influence individual development. "What happens during the first months and years of life matters a lot, not because this period of development provides an indelible blueprint for adult well-being, but because it sets either a sturdy or fragile stage for what follows" (Shonkoff & Phillips, 2000).

Developmentally appropriate practice guides early childhood educators as they provide a child-centered program focusing on the individual needs of each learner (Bredekamp & Copple, 2009). As professional educators, early childhood teachers are engaged in a continuous process of making decisions about learning environments, materials, strategies, and interactions that promote and support early learning. According to Bredekamp and Copple, the core of developmentally appropriate practice lies in *intentionality*—teachers who know the goals for children's learning and who are intentional in helping children achieve these goals. Developmentally appropriate practices are the result of professionals making decisions about the well-being and education of children based on at least three important kinds of knowledge:

1. Knowledge of child development and learning: age-related characteristics, permitting general predictions about what experiences are likely to best promote children's learning and development.
2. Knowledge of each child as an individual: what is learned about each child has implications for how best to adapt responsively to that individual child.

3. Knowledge of the social and cultural contexts in which the children live: values, expectations, and behavioral and linguistic conventions that shape children's lives at home and in their communities. Teachers must strive to understand these contexts in order to ensure that learning experiences in the program are meaningful, relevant, and respectful for each child and family (Bredekamp & Copple, 2009).

Knowledge about human development and how children learn, coupled with knowledge about each individual child, focusing on his or her strengths and interests as well as needs, and knowledge about the families and cultural backgrounds the children come from—all are necessary and critical components of an appropriate, meaningful curriculum and environment for all the children in the class.

Each individual child has a learning style or sensory preference for which he or she is more suited. Learning styles are categorized as visual, auditory, and kinesthetic. Children with visual preferences prefer to learn by sight. Those with auditory preferences prefer activities and learning experiences that include hearing and listening. And those with bodily-kinesthetic preferences prefer to move as they learn. It is important to be aware of our own preferences as adults, because we tend to teach to our own preferences, without intending to do so. Keep in mind other learning styles and preferences and incorporate learning opportunities for all as you design your classroom environments.

In addition to learning styles or preferences, consider multiple intelligences or the many ways that children are smart when designing programs and environments for young children. In Frames of Mind: The Theory of Multiple Intelligences, Howard Gardner explains that an individual acquires a set of specific abilities that are used to solve a problem or create a product within the context of the individual's culture. He asks the question, "How are you smart?" and identifies eight intelligences or ways we are smart: musical, bodily-kinesthetic, logical-mathematical, linguistic, spatial, interpersonal, intrapersonal, and naturalistic. In a child care center, teachers can incorporate this information into every aspect of their environment, curriculum, lesson plans, and daily activities. According to the observations of the teachers in such a center, children are drawn to certain types of activities and thrive in particular areas of the environment because they are strong in specific types of intelligence. The teachers strive to meet the needs of every child and search actively for each child's specific strength and style.

In addition to the children's strengths, staff members have strengths in specific intelligences, and these are reflected in their teaching styles and in the environments they create for children's learning. Consider providing parent education regarding the uniqueness of individual children and the many ways children learn and show they are smart. In the photo below, the staff created a display board about how children are smart. Parents and children learn that all people are smart and that we learn and show what we have learned in many different ways. We are unique human beings, and a well-designed environment provides opportunities for all learning styles and intelligences.

Adapting the Environment for All Learners

Each child is unique, and an effective environment provides a range of materials, activities, and interactions to support all interests and abilities. Classrooms often include children with additional special needs, which may require further adaptations of the classroom environment. Consider the following:

- Children with physical challenges may require wider pathways for wheelchair or walkers, sturdy furniture to assist in pulling up to standing, adaptive seating devices to provide support, and assistive technology.
- Children with speech and language delays may require special tools for communication, such as special word-processing devices, communication boards, and touch pads.
- Children with autism spectrum disorder may require additional verbal symbols to aid communication. A quiet, organized environment that is free from distractions will likely benefit and reduce stress for children with autism.
- Children with developmental delays learn best in environments that are multisensory. Environments that allow small-group or individual work and repetition are supportive for children with cognitive developmental delays.
- Children with behavioral challenges benefit from environments that provide structure and routine. Clear procedures, expectations, and guidelines will often help children remain focused and will increase their engagement. Chairs that rock or swivel, therapy balls, and balance seating often help children with behavioral challenges and can reduce behavior incidents.
- Children who are visually impaired need environments that are brightly lit and provide clear visual information. Touch and sound cues can be used to guide children with visual impairments throughout the room (Isbell & Isbell, 2005).

Chapter 7

The Amazing (and Real)
CLASSROOM MAKEOVER ADVENTURE

The Adventure

You might plan an entire classroom makeover adventure as we did with the kindergarten teacher of this classroom, or you might change a center or two and become inspired to continue and make over your whole space. This was our Amazing (and Real) Classroom Makeover Adventure.

Description of the Classroom

This classroom is located in a small, older elementary school in a rural setting. The school houses seven classrooms, kindergarten to fourth grade. The kindergarten room is self-contained with a wall of windows that lets in abundant natural light. Blinds are used to filter the light when necessary. The floor is tile, and area rugs are used to help define spaces. There is a three-foot-wide storage area that doubles as a coatroom. On one wall is a large bulletin board surface, and on the opposite wall there is an equally large whiteboard surface. Two walls have no electrical outlets. A sink and counter space are located near the storage/coatroom, in what now houses the Art and Science Centers. Bathrooms are located outside the room, down the hall. The school offers special education, art and music, guidance, speech rooms, and a library.

Before

Developing a Vision

Why do you want to change your classroom?

- I am inspired by the schools of Reggio Emilia, Italy, and I would like to implement some of the environmental elements found in these schools. I would like to display materials in aesthetically pleasing ways, especially in the Art Center.
- I would like to use more clear containers and baskets to house materials.
- I would like to have open shelving to display beautiful materials, children's work, photographs, and so on.
- I would also like to define the centers and learning areas better.
- I would like to bring the outdoors in. We live in a beautiful area and have mountains and nature right outside our windows. I would like to incorporate nature and the outdoors into the classroom.
- I would like to use and display more documentation of the learning.
- My overall goal for the classroom environment is for it to be a beautiful place, inviting to children and adults, neat and organized, with live plants and real and natural materials. I would like my classroom to be more home-like.

What do you like about your room?

- The room is neat and organized.
- The children feel at home in the classroom.
- We have a good meeting/"rug time" area. The children and I can meet here and work together.
- There are windows in front of the room.

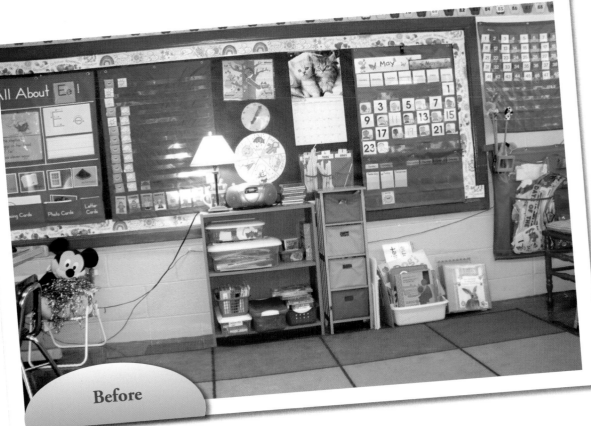

Before

What would you like to change in the classroom?

- I would like more clearly defined centers.
- The Book Center needs to be better organized for children to access the books. I would like neutral colors for the room (calm colors of autumn).
- I would like an alternative to the harsh lighting.
- I would like to move away from a school environment to a more natural, home-like setting.
- I also would like the coatroom to be better organized.

The Change Process

Following this initial interview, the teacher and the authors determined the key elements of the transformation. Chapter 1 describes the elements of design to consider when creating a quality place for young children and their teachers:

- Beauty in Everyday Environments (aesthetic environment)
- The Impact of Light (visual environment)
- Sounds Make a Difference (auditory environment)
- A Place for Everything, Everything in its Place (functional environment)
- A Secure and Supportive Environment (nurturing environment)
- Valuing Diversity in the Classroom (environments that value diversity)
- Setting Up Appropriate Learning Environments (learning environment)

Together, the authors and the teacher determined which of thse elements would be the focus of this Amazing (and *Real*) Classroom Makeover, selecting the aesthetic, the functional, and the learning environments..

The First Element of Design Considered: Beauty in Everyday Environments (aesthetic environment)

Plan of Action

- Determine wall color.
- Determine accent color for furniture and borders.
- Paint all furniture.

- Clean and declutter the classroom to remove excess materials and minimize items in storage.
- Reduce the number of bright colors.
- Swap the existing rug for a more neutral tone.

The Next Element of Design Considered: A Place for Everything, Everything in Its Place (functional environment)

The functional environment is how the classroom design incorporates a variety of spaces to meet the needs of individuals and the group. Consider the fixed features, such as the sink, windows, and outlets, and map out a plan for the space. The goal for the functional environment is to design a room arrangement that works for children and adults. In addition to furniture and learning centers, think about materials, storage, and display. Materials should be well organized and accessible and should encourage responsibility and exploration. Storage and display should attract children and encourage them to make choices and be responsible for the proper use and return of materials. During the planning phase, we discussed ridding the room of excess materials and storage items that were rarely used and were cluttering the space. In this makeover, the teacher removed surplus materials, freeing up the space to create a new learning environment.

Plan of Action

- Determine goals for the children.
- Consider how the design of the environment can help children reach the goals.
- Determine which centers to include.
- Draw a map of the room arrangement.
- Determine which materials are to be included in each center area.
- Determine which materials to keep in storage for later use.
- Determine which materials are to be recycled or discarded.

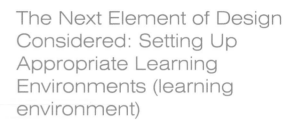

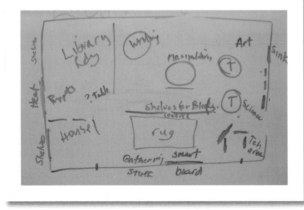

The Next Element of Design Considered: Setting Up Appropriate Learning Environments (learning environment)

The learning environment is the third element of design focus for this makeover. When planning for change, keep in mind early learning standards (curriculum guidelines), areas of development (cognitive, language/literacy, social/emotional, physical/motor), unique needs (individual needs/interests, social/cultural influences, learning styles, and intelligences), and any special needs and adaptations for children.

Teacher Interview and Reflection on the Learning Environment

What are the goals for the children in your classroom?

The goals for the children in my classroom are as follows:

- To understand the curriculum that they are to learn according to the state kindergarten curriculum standards;
- To do their personal best and reach individual goals;
- To form close relationships with the teacher and other children in the classroom;
- To enjoy working, learning, and playing in their "home away from home;"
- To gain a lifelong love and desire for learning.

How do you want the children to use the space to accomplish the goals?

I want the children to use the space to accomplish these goals in the following ways:

- To investigate and explore their own ideas and interests;
- To work with others and learn from each other;
- To use materials in many ways and to test their ideas and interests;
- To relax in the environment provided, to feel comfortable in the environment, and to know that the space is their own;
- To add to the environment their own work, constructions, art, and ideas.

What are your reflections during this part of the process?

Reggio-inspired rooms are not cluttered and have a soft, natural look. When cleaning the classroom, I found things that I did not even know I had. That told me that I should get rid of them, because I was not using them. We cleaned storage areas, cabinets, and closets to make room for items that need to be stored, remembering the overall goal of reducing the quantity of materials in the classroom, especially unused materials. I removed my large teacher desk. That made room for another center. It is all hard work but worth it.

The teacher and authors developed a plan to make over several aspects of the classroom learning environment, focusing on organizing and equipping centers that afford children opportunities to learn, practice, and refine their knowledge and skills. They created a plan of action for each center, keeping in mind learning standards, which were emphasized as children naturally played with learning. The following plans of action and photos show the transformation of each center.

Art

Before

Plan of Action

- Reduce the number of stimulating, bright colors (red, orange, yellow, bright green).
- Use natural and earth tones (beige, brown, soft green).
- Use lower shelving to store and display materials.
- Organize materials on shelves for easy access.
- Add paint easels of various sizes.
- Use clear containers and baskets to organize materials.
- Display works of art (photos, drawings, paintings, sculptures).
- Add books about art, museums, color, and artists.

The goal for the functional environment is to design a room arrangement that meets the needs of children and adults.

Standards Addressed During Play in the Art Center

According to Tennessee state educational standards (state.tn.us/education/ci/arts/doc/ART_VA_K.pdf), children in kindergarten should learn to:

- Use selected tools and materials in a safe manner to create a work of art;
- Apply a variety of techniques and processes to produce original works of art that reflect personal experiences, imagination, and observations;
- Demonstrate an understanding that all people can express themselves visually;
- Demonstrate an understanding that subject matter can be real or imaginary.

Before

Plan of Action

- Create a larger, more comfortable area for reading.
- Display books in a variety of attractive ways (bookshelf showing front covers of books, shelving showing spines, shelves for puppets and other items related to the books on display).
- Organize books on shelves for easy access.
- Add a tent to define the reading space.
- Provide soft items such as pillows and rugs inside the tent for comfortable reading.
- Add clipboards, pencils, and paper for writing and retelling stories through pictures.

After

Standards Addressed During Play in the Book Center

According to the Common Core Standards (corestandards.org), with prompting and support, children in kindergarten should learn to:

- Ask and answer questions about texts;
- Retell stories;
- Identify story characters, settings, and major events in a story;
- Ask and answer questions about words in text;
- Recognize a variety of common texts (storybooks, poems);
- Name the author and illustrator of a story;
- Define the role of the author and illustrator of a story;
- Describe the relationship between illustrations and the story;
- Compare and contrast the adventures and experiences of characters in familiar stories;
- Actively engage in group reading activities with purpose and understanding.

Blocks

Plan of Action

- Create more space for children to work with blocks.
- Use the rug in the gathering space as an area for block play.
- Organize materials on shelves for easy access.
- Encourage independence and responsibility by labeling shelves and bins so children know where materials belong.
- Provide a variety of blocks (large and small).
- Add tape measures, pencils, paper, and clipboards.

Before

After

Standards Addressed During Play in the Block Center

According to the Common Core Standards (corestandards.org), children in kindergarten should learn to:

- Know number names and count sequence;
- Count to tell the number of objects;
- Describe and compare measurable attributes;
- Classify objects and count the number of objects in categories;
- Identify and describe shapes (squares, circles, triangles, rectangles, hexagons, cubes, cones, cylinders, and spheres);
- Identify shapes as two-dimensional or three-dimensional;
- Analyze, compare, create, and compose shapes.

Gathering Place

Before

Plan of Action

- Reduce the number of bright, stimulating colors.
- Add soft neutral tones to the walls and rugs.
- Organize and display items for easy access for children.
- Plan for multiple uses of the gathering area (i.e., blocks).
- **Note:** During the classroom makeover a Smartboard was added to the bulletin board surface in the gathering place.

After

Standards Addressed During Play in the Gathering Area

According to the Common Core Standards (corestandards.org), children in kindergarten should learn to:

- Participate in collaborative conversations with diverse partners about kindergarten topics and texts with peers and adults;
- Follow agreed-upon rules for discussions, such as listening to others and taking turns speaking;
- Ask and answer questions about key details of a text read aloud or other information presented orally or through other media;
- Ask and answer questions to seek help, obtain information, or clarify information presented in the large group;
- Describe familiar people, places, things, events;
- Share drawings or other visual displays to provide additional detail;
- Speak audibly and express thoughts, feelings, and ideas clearly.

Center Drawing: Gathering Place

Home Living

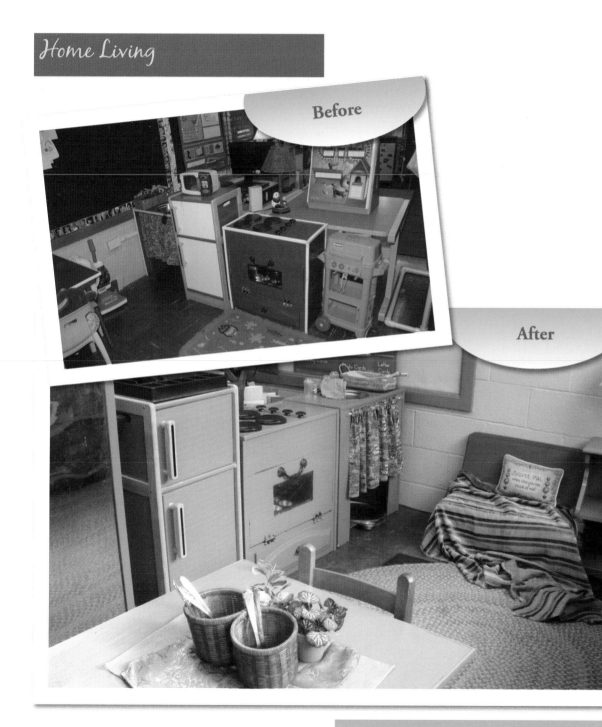

Before

After

Plan of Action

- Reduce the number of bright, stimulating colors.
- Add soft neutral tones to the walls and rugs.
- Organize and display items for easy access for children.
- Add authentic items.
- Add a table for eating and preparing food as the central focus.
- Add soft seating and lamps for a more homelike atmosphere.
- Add literacy tools, such as pads, pencils, small whiteboards, magazines, and books to read to babies.

Standards Addressed During Play in the Home Living Center

According to Tennessee state education standards (tennessee.gov/education/ci/ss/doc/SS_Grade_K.pdf), children in kindergarten should learn to:

- Understand the diversity of human cultures;
- Understand that some differences among people are a result of their culture;
- Indentify similarities and differences in food, clothes, homes, games, and families in different cultures;
- Compare family customs and traditions among cultures.

Before

Plan of Action

- Add open shelving to display materials.
- Add clear containers and baskets to store materials.
- Add plants and fish to care for.
- Add science journals for note-taking and documentation.

Standards Addressed During Play in the Science Center

According to Tennessee state education standards (tn.gov/education/ci/sci/doc/SCI_Grade_K.pdf), children in kindergarten will learn to:

- Observe the world of familiar objects using the senses and tools;
- Ask questions, make logical predictions, plan investigations, and represent data;
- Recognize that many things are made of parts;
- Recognize that some things are living and some are not;
- Know that people interact with their environment through their senses;
- Recognize that living things require water, food, and air;
- Recognize that some objects are man-made and that some occur naturally;
- Describe an object by its observable properties.

After

Before

Plan of Action

- Add shelving to create a defined writing center.
- Add baskets to store a variety of items for writing.
- Use a clear plastic shoe holder to create mailboxes for individual children.
- Add a variety of writing tools.
- Include table space, clipboards and whiteboards for practice writing.
- Add resources such as dictionaries, books, sample writings, and stories teachers and children have composed.

Standards Addressed During Play in the Writing Center

According to the Common Core Standards (corestandards.org), children in kindergarten should learn to:

- Use a combination of drawing, dictating, and writing to represent opinions about the text;
- Use a combination of drawing, dictating, and writing to compose information and explanatory texts;
- Use a combination of drawing, dictating, and writing to narrate an event and add reaction;
- Know and apply grade-level phonics and word-analysis skills;
- Print many uppercase and lowercase letters;
- Recognize and name end punctuation;
- Spell simple words phonetically, drawing on knowledge of sound-letter relationships.

After

Summary

Which elements of design would you focus on, if you engaged in your own Amazing (and *Real*) Classroom Makeover?

We chose to focus on the aesthetic environment, the functional environment, and the learning environment.

The results:
- Clearly defined centers
- Less clutter, fewer excess materials
- Fewer stimulating colors
- Calm, neutral tones
- Organized, easily accessible materials
- Authentic materials
- Multiple materials for choice in centers
- Enhanced opportunities for engagement in the learning process

Before

Teacher Comments
After the Makeover

Before the Beginning of School

- The room looks so different, and the centers are very well defined.
- I really wanted a classroom environment that would encourage children to work actively together, and the room is now set up in that way.
- I wanted to get rid of the "commercial classroom" look and create a Reggio-inspired, home-like environment. I think there is more that can be done in the room to contribute to this, such as adding more live plants, adding more alternative lighting, adding curtains or valances on the windows, and putting away more of the materials, to create interest in the materials displayed in the centers.

Midyear

- The centers are better defined, and the children stay and work longer, instead of running around from center to center.
- I see a huge difference; color makes a huge difference. The children are calmer.
- Having fewer materials is actually better. The children can get things out independently and put things away on their own. They stay more focused on their work.
- The children love having clipboards to use around the room. They [clipboards] are easy to transport and encourage writing around the room.
- Adding a fish to the Science Center has created excitement and interest as well as increased literacy opportunities. The children have decided they

After

need to read to the fish and show the fish pictures of itself found in the science books located in the center.

- The children use the Art Center well. The materials are displayed and labeled well for easy identification and access.
- At first the tent in the Reading Center caused some trouble because the children were more interested in using it in their socio-dramatic play around a camping theme. After spending time introducing the proper use of the center, the children focused on reading.
- The mailboxes in the Writing Center are awesome. The children this year are writing a lot!
- Home Living has to be one of the favorite centers. Many kindergarten classrooms don't include home living as a center. The children learn so much in the Home Living Center, especially in the area of language development.
- The children aren't the only ones who have commented on the room. Parents commented as well. One comment from a parent was "This is a dream come true!"

After

Final Reflection

- The makeover has increased learning opportunities for the children by more clearly defining areas of the classroom.
- Having fewer materials also helps the children choose and not feel overwhelmed. The room setup allows the children to move freely from place to place and provides more opportunities for cooperative learning and activities.
- There are literacy opportunities for children in every center.
- Increased learning opportunities in **writing**—The Writing Center is a separate center (it was previously combined with the Art Center), and it is better organized. There is a greater variety of materials for the children to choose from, and they now have mailboxes to share notes and pictures with each other. The children use the center more after the makeover.
- Increased learning opportunities in **blocks**—The clear bins enable the children to see the available materials. The big block shelf is much better for storage. The different blocks are now stored neatly, and all the same block types are together. The new labels also help with literacy.
- Increased learning opportunities in **science**—The science area was very small and stored on a moving cart before the makeover. Now it is a clearly defined space and the materials allow the children to explore their ideas. The children are learning more because they utilize materials and have a better space for this exploration to extend their learning.
- Increased learning opportunities in **art**—The Art Center is now set up in a more interesting and beautiful way, which draws the children into the center. The materials are stored in clear containers and baskets so the children can see and use the materials in a greater variety of ways. I think the natural materials also invite the children to explore ideas they would not have previously.
- Increased learning opportunities in **books**—The children are visiting the Library Center much more now that the books are better organized, and they can find what they want to read. The tent draws the children to the center as well. I think the children are having more reading experiences due to the changes. They are also gaining comprehension skills from the listening area of the Library Center.
- Increased learning opportunities in **home living**—The children have always loved the Home Living Center, but there are now many more literacy experiences provided and used. The children have phone books, notepads, checkbooks, and books to read to the "children," and many more literacy-related items. The children are reading and writing more and gaining better literacy skills from these additions to home living.

Whether you decide to work alone or in partnership with others, enjoy the adventure! What will your Amazing (and *Real*) Classroom Makeover look like?

References

Bodrova, E. & Leong, D.J. 2007. *Tools of the mind: The Vygotskian approach to early childhood education, 2nd edition*. Upper Saddle River, NJ: Pearson Merrill Prentice Hall.

Bredekamp, S. & Copple, C., eds. 2009. *Developmentally appropriate practice in early childhood programs, 3rd edition*. Washington, DC: National Association for the Education of Young Children.

Common Core State Standards Initiative. http://www.corestandards.org/ (accessed October 18, 2011).

Gardner, H. 1983. *Frames of mind: The theory of multiple intelligences*. New York: Basic Books.

Greenman, Jim. 2007. *Caring spaces, learning places: Children's environments that work*. Redmond, WA: Exchange Press.

Harms, T., Clifford, R. M., & Cryer, D. 2005. *Early childhood environment rating scale,* revised edition. New York: Teachers College Press.

Isbell, C. & Isbell, R. 2005. *The inclusive learning center book for preschool children with special needs*. Beltsville, MD: Gryphon House.

Isbell, R, 2008. *The complete learning center book,* revised. Beltsville, MD: Gryphon House.

Jensen, E. 2005. *Teaching with the brain in mind,* 2nd edition. Alexandria, VA: Association for Supervision and Curriculum Development.

Katz, L.G. 1999. Another look at what young children should be learning. ERIC Digest. Champaign, IL: ERIC Clearinghouse on Elementary and Early Childhood Education. ED 380 735.

Morrow, L.M. 1990. "Preparing the classroom environment to promote literacy during play." *Early Childhood Research Quarterly* 5: 537–554.

National Association for the Education of Young Children. 2002. *Early learning standards: Creating the conditions for success* (position statement). Washington, DC: NAEYC.

National Science Teachers Association. 1996. *National Science Education Standards*. http://www.nsta.org/publications/nses.aspx (accessed September 20, 2010).

Neuman, S.B. & Roskos, K. 1992. "Literary objects as cultural tools: Effects on children's literacy behaviors." *Reading Research Quarterly* 27(3):202–225.

Olds, A. 2000. *Child care design guide*. New York: McGraw-Hill.

Pianta, R. C., LaParo, K. M., & Hamre, B. K. 2008. *Classroom assessment scoring system™* (CLASS™) Baltimore, MD: Paul H. Brookes Publishing Co.

Plutro, M. 2000. "Planning for linguistic and cultural diversity: Curriculum in Head Start." *Head Start Bulletin*. U.S. Department for Health and Human Services/Administration for Children and Families/Administration for Children, Youth, and Families/Healthcare Systems Bureau, 67:19–21.

Pre-K Teachers Resource Center. (n.d.) "Meeting standards." preknow.org/educators/resource/meetingstandards.cfm.

Shonkoff, J. & Phillips, D., eds., 2000. *Neurons to neighborhoods: The science of early childhood development*. Washington, DC: National Academy of Sciences.

Smilansky, S. & Shefatya, L. 1990. *Facilitating play: A medium for promoting cognitive, socio-emotional and academic development in young children*. Gaithersburg, MD: Psychosocial and Educational Publications.

Smith, M. W., Brady, J. P., & Anastasopoulos, L. 2008. *The early childhood language and literacy classroom observation tool, Pre-K.* Baltimore, MD: Paul H. Brookes Publishing Co.

Smith, M. W., Brady, J. P., & Clark-Chiarelli, N. 2008. *The early childhood language and literacy classroom observation tool, K–3,* research edition. Baltimore, MD: Paul H. Brookes Publishing Co.

Tennessee Department of Education. (n.d.). "Early Childhood/Early Learning Developmental Standards." http://tn.gov/education/ci/earlychildhood/index.shtml (accessed September 2, 2010).

Tennessee Department of Education. (n.d.) "Science Curriculum Standards." http://tn.gov/education/ci/sci/doc/SCI_Grade_K.pdf. (accessed October 18, 2011).

Tennessee Department of Education. (n.d.) "Social Studies Curriculum Standards." http://tn.gov/education/ci/ss/doc/SS_Grade_K.pdf (accessed October 18, 2011).

Tennessee Department of Education. (n.d.) "Visual Art Curriculum Standards Kindergarten." http://state.tn.us/education/ci/arts/doc/ART_VA_K.pdf. (accessed October 18, 2011).

Vukelich, C. 1991. "Where's the paper? Literacy during dramatic play." *Childhood Education* 66: 205–209.

Walsh, G. & Gardner, J. 2005. "Assessing the quality of early years learning environments." *Early Childhood Research and Practice.* Spring 2005 Volume 7 Number 1: 1–18.

Classroom Evaluation Checklist

The following questions can help you think about your classroom and consider possibilities as you work to create a beautiful and effective environment for teachers and children. It can also help you assess the progress toward your desired environment as you engage in the process of change.

○ When a child enters your classroom, does he or she see a warm and inviting place?

○ Does every child see attractively displayed pictures of all the children who live in this community?

○ What are the sounds the child hears when he or she is in the space?

○ Do the classroom environment and materials demonstrate what is valued in this place?

○ Are pictures of the children's involvement and examples of their work displayed so they can be admired by the children, parents, teachers, and other adults?

○ Are a variety of areas available: quiet, active, messy, and large or small group? Can the children easily see where these areas are located?

○ Are materials grouped together and close to where they will be used, nurturing children's independence?

○ Are the materials and the space clearly organized so children can easily select the items they need for their work?

○ Are open-ended materials included in the space to challenge children's creative thinking?

○ Is there a place for children to pause, to be calm, and to reflect?

○ Are beautiful items and natural materials displayed to be enjoyed?

○ Is there a place to store the teacher's personal items?

○ Are there places to sit comfortably?

○ Is it possible to identify the special adults and their interests in this space by their personal displays?

○ Is the lighting varied and controllable in the space that is being changed or the new space being planned?

○ Does this new feature or classroom area function effectively with the other components of the classroom?

○ Does the environment provide opportunities for children and adults to "play" with learning, and explore, reflect on, and share learning experiences?

Index

A
aesthetics, 9–12
Art Centers, 87–91, 131–132, 147
artists, 11
artwork
    Art Center makeover, 87–91, 131–132
    and cognitive development, 20
    designated spaces for, 15
    use of, in classroom environments, 10–11
auditory learning style, 125
auditory stimulation, 13
    See also sounds
autism, 126

B
beauty, 9–12
belonging, sense of, 41
blocks, in Construction Centers, 57–60
Blocks Center, 61–64, 135–136
bodily-kinesthetic learning style, 125
Bodrova, E., 44
books
    in Art Center, 90
    in Calming Area, 118
    in Construction Centers, 59
    in Fire Station Center, 99
    in Home Living Center, 94
    and language/literacy development, 20
    in learning centers, 45
    in Library Centers, 52, 147
    in Literacy Center, 55
    in Manipulatives Area Center, 67
    in safe spaces, 17
    in Science Center, 81
    storage, 46
    storage of, 41, 133
    in Water Center, 70
See also language and literacy development; Library
    Centers; Literacy Centers

brainstorming, 23
Bredekamp, S., 124–125

C
Calming Place, 17, 117–121
canopy, 47–48
child development
    and learning standards, 124–125
    stages in, 19–22
children
    classroom environment's impact on, 7
    learning styles of, 124–125
    lighting's impact on, 13
    multiple intelligences of, 125
    personal spaces for, 15, 41
    photos of, 107, 116
    preparing for new classroom features, 27–28
    providing choices for, 42
    and responsibility, 40
    sounds' impact on, 13
    special needs, 46, 126
    valuing as community member, 38
    See also large groups; play; small groups
choices, 42
Classroom Assessment Scoring System (CLASS), 24
classroom environments
    aesthetics of, 9
    and cognitive development, 19–20
    color's impact on, 10–11
    communication spaces in, 17
    designated spaces in, 15–16
    design elements to consider in, 9–18, 129, 151
    emotional support in, 16–17
    flexibility in, 16
    and functionality, 130
    impact on children, 7
    impact on learning, 130
    impact on teachers, 7
    introducing new features, 27–28

and language/literacy development, 20
lighting in, 13
low-cost improvements to, 29–34
Olds' recommendations for, 15
and physical/motor development, 22
planning process for changing, 23–26
plants in, 12
safe spaces in, 17
and sense of community, 35–42
and social/emotional development, 21
clutter, 24, 29, 34, 131
cognitive development, 19–20
color, and classroom environment, 10–11
Common Core Standards, 134, 143
community, sense of, 35–42, 106–107
computers. See Literacy Centers
Construction Center, 57–60
Copple, C., 124–125
cubbies, 15, 41

D
decluttering, 24, 29, 34, 131
design
    beauty's role in, 9–12, 129
    checklist, 26, 151
    elements to consider in, 9–18, 129
    and functionality, 13–16, 130
    and learning, 130
    and supportive environments, 16–17
disabilities, 46, 126
distractions, minimizing, 39–40, 107
diversity, 18–19, 39, 138–139

E
Early Childhood Environment Rating Scale, Revised
    (ECERS-R) tool, 24
Early Language and Literacy Classroom Observation
    (ELLCO) tool, 24

emotional development. See social and emotional
    development
emotional support, 16–17, 21
entryways, 35–36, 111–116
environments. See classroom environments

F
fabric
    in Calming Area, 121
    in Gathering Place, 107
    library canopy, 46, 48
    library tent, 49–52
    low-cost improvements using, 30–31
    for noise absorption, 59
    and Science Center, 80
    in Water Center, 71–72
families
    and diversity, 18–19
    valuing as community members, 39
Fire Station Center, 97–100
flexibility, 16
flowers, 12
fluorescent lights, 13
functionality, 130

G
Gardner, Howard, 125
Gathering Place Center, 106–110, 137–138
grandparents, 39
Greenman, Jim, 35
groups. See large groups; small groups

H
Harms, T., 24
Hofmann, Hans, 90
Home Living Centers, 43–44, 92–96, 139, 147

I
Individual Education Plans (IEPs), 46
instruments. See Music and Performance Center
intelligences, multiple, 125
intentionality, 124
Isbell, C., 126
Isbell, R., 19, 43, 126

J
Jensen, E., 21

K
Katz, L.G., 23–24
kinesthetic learning style, 125
knowledge, types of, 124–125

L
language and literacy development
    in Block Centers, 61
    Books Center makeover, 133–134
    classroom tools for, 20
    in Construction Centers, 57, 59
    and Early Language and Literacy Classroom
        Observation (ELLCO) tool, 24
    in Home Living Center, 94, 147
    and learning centers, 45
    in Library Centers, 46–52
    in Literacy Centers, 53–56
    in Restaurant Center, 101, 105
    in Writing Center, 142–143, 147
large groups
    and Gathering Place, 106–107
    and language/literacy development, 20
    and sense of community, 39–40
learners. See children
learning centers, and play, 43–44
learning objectives, 123
learning standards
    and Art Centers, 132

and Block Centers, 136
and Book Centers, 134
Common Core Standards, 134, 138, 143
and Gathering Place, 138
and Home Living Centers, 139
overview of, 123–124
and Science Centers, 141
Tennessee State Standards, 132, 139, 141
learning styles, 125
Leong, D.J., 44
Library Centers
    canopy makeover, 46–48
    classroom makeover, 133–134
    tent, 49–52
lighting
    in Gathering Place, 107
    ideas for adding, 80
    use of, in classroom environments, 13
literacy. See language and literacy development
Literacy Centers, 53–56
low-cost changes, 29–34

M
mailboxes, 56, 147
makeovers
    for Art Studio Center, 87–91
    for Blocks Center, 61–64
    for Calming Area, 117–121
    "before" classroom description, 127
    for Construction Center, 57–60
    for Fire Station, 97–100
    for Gathering Place, 106–110
    goals for classroom, 128
    for Home Living Center, 92–96
    for Library Centers, 46–52
    for Literacy Area, 53–56
    for Manipulatives Center, 65–68
    for Math Center, 74–77

    for Music/Performance Center, 82–86
    for Restaurant Center, 101–105
    for Science Center, 78–81
    teacher comments after, 145
    for Water Center, 69–73
    for Welcome Area, 111–116
manipulatives, in Math Center, 74–77
Manipulatives Center, 65–68
Math Center, 74–77
motor development. See physical and motor development
multiculturalism, 18–19, 39, 139
multiple intelligences, 125
Music and Performance Center, 82–86

N
National Association for the Education of Young Children (NAEYC), 123–124
National Association of Early Childhood Specialists in State Departments of Education (NAECS/SDE), 124
natural materials. See Science Center
noise. See sounds

O
objectives, learning, 123–124
Olds, A., 13, 15
organizing, 24
    See also decluttering; storage
overhead projector, 59–60
overstimulation, 17, 29

P
paint, use of, in classroom environments, 10
parents, 39
Peace Center, 17
Phillips, D., 124
photos, 107, 116

physical and motor development
    classroom tools for, 22
    Manipulatives Center, 65–68
    and manipulatives in Math Center, 74–77
Pianta, R.C., 24
pictures. See artwork; photos
place, sense of, 37
plants, 12
play
    as learning tool, 43–45
    See also specific learning centers
Plutro, M., 18

R
reading, lighting for, 13
recording studio, 84
Reggio Emilia, 10, 107, 128, 131, 145
responsibility, learning about, 40
Restaurant Center, 101–105
routines, 21, 40

S
safe spaces, 17
sand tables, 69–70
Science Center, 78–81, 140–141, 147
Shefatya, L., 43
Shonkoff, J., 124
small groups
    and language/literacy development, 20
    and play, 43
    and sense of community, 42
Smilanksy, S., 43
Smith, M.W., 24
social and emotional development
    and Calming Area, 117–118, 121
    in safe spaces, 17
    supported by classroom environments, 21

sounds
    controlling, 14, 59, 62
    impact of, on children, 13
spaces. *See* classroom environments
special needs, 46, 126
staff members, 39
stage, constructing, 84
standards, learning. See learning standards
storage
    Art Center makeover, 89
    blocks, 62–64, 147
    books, 133–134
    of children's work, 41
    enhancing visually, 30
    in Gathering Place, 107
    in Home Living Center, 94
    manipulatives, 66–68, 74–77
    Water Center tools, 71
students. *See* children

T

teachers
    on classroom makeovers, 145
    impact of classroom environment on, 7
    observation by, 21, 25
    spaces for, 32, 34
    valuing as community members, 38
Tennessee State Standards, 132, 139, 141
tent, 49–52
theater. See Music and Performance Center

U

umbrellas, 77

V

visual interest
    fabric, 71–72
    mobiles, 118
    umbrellas, 77
visual learning style, 125
vocabulary, expanding through choice of design
    elements, 9

W

Water Center, 69–73
Welcome Area, 111–116
Writing Center, 142–143, 147
writing materials
    and language/literacy development, 20
    in learning centers, 45
    and physical/motor development, 22
    See also language and literacy development